ANGELIKA KILIAN

You Can Have It All

30 STEPS TO BECOMING THE BEST VERSION OF YOURSELF AND LIVING YOUR DREAM LIFE

You Can Have It All

30 Steps to Becoming
the Best Version of Yourself
and Living Your Dream Life

Angelika Kilian

GREEN HEART
LIVING
—PRESS—

You Can Have It All

ISBN Paperback: 978-1-954493-57-5

Published by Green Heart Living Press

This is a work of creative nonfiction. The events are portrayed to the best of the author's memory. While all the stories in this book are true, some names and identifying details have been changed to protect the privacy of the people involved.

Dedication

To my old self.

Contents

Welcome

I decided to change my life.

I wanted to improve everything about myself and become the high-quality woman I always dreamt of. I began to envision myself as strong, independent, and successful.

To accomplish this, I needed to put myself first. I needed to allow the old me to die, and welcome the new me: the Real Angelika Kilian—a beautiful, divine feminine Queen living her dream life.

In this workbook, I will share my stories of transformation and provide you with guidance and tools to welcome in your authentic self and live your dream life.

Always with love,

-1-

Reprogram Your Mind

Step 1: Reprogram Your Mind

In order to change ourselves and become successful we have to change the way we think or were programmed to think. We have to change the way we react to things. Change the way we speak. Change the way we behave. Change the old patterns that limited us and reprogram new healthy successful patterns. Change the thoughts of *we do not have enough money* to *I have riches*. Change the mindset of *do not ask for anything when we walk into the store* to *let's explore and when the time comes we will purchase it*. It's a way of giving hope and focusing on positive thinking.

How about *don't touch this* to *here is something else you can play with*? Give yourself options. Explore the good before the negative, but still address the negative. It's all in the new approach. Oh, how I had to relearn this!

Think of the way we are programmed to talk to each other—the programmed, "Hi, how are, you?" "Good and you?" Or "Have a nice day." "Thanks, you too." Yes, these exchanges are programmed into our subconscious. It's a natural reaction.

Now, let's reprogram this into the authentic and more personal you.

"Hey, how are you?"

Response: "Thanks for asking. I am great, just had my morning coffee." This may give the asker a reminder to have their coffee or something to drink, so it may even give some positive feedback that you didn't even know you were giving.

I remember I called the Encore Management office one day and as I asked this gentleman how he was doing today he responded "Fantastic!"

Damn, did this grab my attention! Being on the phone with him actually put a smile on my face. If he was feeling fantastic, I wanted to be feeling fantastic too. It was such a higher, positive energy that I was attracted to. I do not remember the whole conversation, but let me tell you after that phone call ended I felt so much positive energy.

I know this might feel a little silly, but it's starting at the basics to understand change.

Let's try again:
"Have a nice day." I always like to answer, "Thank you, it will be the Best Day ever." I am setting up my intention of having the best day ever. So anything that will happen will be the best for me. Even when bad things happen, trust me these are blessings in disguise.

The person that hears me say this is probably thinking either, *Wow, she is so positive,* or agreeing with me, *Yes, it will be the best day ever.* A little change in our daily dialogue can lead to many changes and new outcomes. It all starts in your mind.

In order to get there we have to understand the brain's function of conscious vs. subconscious thinking in order to know how it works so you know how to change it. Knowledge is a powerful thing.

Let's get started. Your subconscious thoughts help you take care of your basic daily functioning. Basic tasks that you do not need to think about before you do them. Like opening a door when you enter a place. Putting toothpaste on your toothbrush. Chewing your food before you swallow. It also relates to your "fight and flight" reaction and stores the things you learn like sports and music. This becomes second nature.

Our subconscious is also responsible for our experiences and knowledge forming our memory. It stores the way we think and feel about these past experiences. Mostly our subconscious helps us navigate the world efficiently. Sometimes we might develop unhealthy habits or attitudes that can prevent us from achieving our goals. This is where conscious thinking can benefit us.

Your conscious thinking is higher thinking, where we can be more considerate of what we think, feel, or do. We can use our conscious thinking to reprogram our subconscious thinking to help change our thoughts, attitudes, and habits. Conscious thinking allows us to take more control over our brains and achieve our goals.

This type of thinking was programmed into you. You absorbed this type of thinking between your birth and seven years old. After seven, you become more conscious of your surroundings and take part in more decision-making, and become your individual self.

This hit me deeply when I learned this. I mean damn, the things that I experienced, saw, felt, and reacted to as a child during those ages. It had me literally shaking my head. I still remember certain events and values. This is why many people experience the effects of childhood trauma way into adulthood.

I had to reprogram my whole subconscious. My whole belief system. My thoughts. I had to figure out the difference between emotions and feelings and how they work together. I had to learn how to handle them. To accept them. To live them. To process them. To handle the anxiety that came with them and try not to react. Understand myself more. Understand why certain things happen. I had to reprogram my subconscious mind to react, respond, and think in different ways. To talk in different ways: positive, affirmative, and with confidence. To walk a certain way. (Yes, your presence in a room speaks about you.) Oh, how wonderful it was changing to the person, the woman, I was destined to be.

It all starts with your willpower to change. Are you ready to change? Are you ready to be the successful person you always dreamed of being? Are you ready to live your dream life? Are you ready to become the best version of yourself so you can attract your dream life? Well, it all starts with you!

At age 32, I finally let go and released my old subconscious patterns that held onto my suffering and pain that only produced the same negative results.

I reprogrammed my subconscious mind to respond differently to the world, people, and things around me in order to produce a different outcome in my life. A successful outcome is coming to me by my becoming the person I always dreamed of. Through this transformation, I was introduced to a new way of thinking that continuously brings me closer to my goals, dreams, and success.

Once you can reprogram your subconscious mind and be conscious, you will get the results you want. Control your thoughts, control your life.

I am here to show you how.

Below are four exercises that will guide you to understand how you can reprogram your mind and live the life you want. You will find more exercises throughout this book as you continue to read.

 *Exercise 1*

Write everything that is present around you, starting with:

"I am here sitting/standing/ lying on _____
There is _____ in front of me.
There is _____ on the floor.
I am feeling _____

In your journal, write more about your surroundings.

You have now completed the first task of controlling your mind by focusing on the present things around you.

 *Exercise 2*

Watch this video:

Now research the subconscious and conscious mind.

Remember you are what you invest your time in. So, either invest your time researching the conscious and subconscious mind or go look at your social media and waste time. Your choice. Now start researching and start writing what you find out. This is another way of reprogramming your subconscious: writing it down. By writing your new knowledge down, you are learning and reprogramming your mind.

 *Exercise 3*

Reprogram your old beliefs with affirmations, meditation, and motivational speakers. You can begin by watching the video below.

Remember this takes time to reprogram your unconscious mind. You have been programmed to think a certain way throughout your lifetime, and now you are striving for change. Be patient with yourself, and stay consistent in practicing listening to these.

Remember this is your journey to become the best version of yourself. Things do not happen overnight. Be persistent about it.

 *Exercise 4*

Become conscious and live in the present moment. Use your new subconscious beliefs and put them into action. This will take willpower to control your thoughts. See the examples below.

Example:

Old belief: You are crazy, you need a psychiatrist.

New belief: I am healthy, but just stored a lot of trauma. (Subconscious)

Willpower: Get a therapist. Eat healthy. Exercise. (Conscious)

Example:

Old belief: I have no friends. Everyone has turned against me.

New belief: They were not true friends and did not play a healthy part in my life.

Willpower: I will meet the right people along my journey to support my mental health and my dreams.

Write down some old beliefs you want to get rid of and how you can create a new positive belief. Implant this new belief into your subconscious. New beliefs, new goals, new you. You are now purely conscious and aware of what you want.

-2-

Create a Vision

Step 2: Create a Vision

Creating a vision of your life is essential. Create a vivid mental image of what you want your business or yourself to be at some point in the future, based on your goals and aspirations.

You have to see it to believe it. Do you know what you want? A vision board allows you to see things for the future. Allows you to see them in front of you. Allows you to see them and create an internal feeling like you already have them.

Now go and google the vision you created. Find the images on the internet, in magazines, or take pictures in stores. Create a place for them in your home. Somewhere you can see constantly. If they are in your phone, add these items to a specific folder or your "favorites." Make them your screensaver. The point is to see these items as often as possible.

I always wanted to purchase my first home, a multi-family home side by side. It was time to start looking. (Even though many people said, "It's not time, the market is not good right now to purchase." Blah, blah, blah.)

Here are the specifics about the property I wanted:

- A two-family home that was side by side.
- Near the ocean.
- A fixer-upper would be ok since my ex-husband is a professional and amazing contractor.
- Top school districts for my sons.
- A decent size yard.

The first step toward the goal: We went looking. The first property was in Braintree. The whole house needed renovation. I was so overwhelmed that I had to leave. Also, it had a very small yard. Definite no.

The second house was $200K over our budget, but I still wanted to have the experience of seeing how it feels to be inside an expensive house. It was a double family, side by side, with ocean views. So we went. OMG this place was enormous. A total of six bathrooms, eight bedrooms, two kitchens, a garage, a barroom, and a good amount of land. Almost 5,000 square feet. The true meaning of a mansion. I think it took about an hour to walk through the whole house. I was impressed. The woodwork inside, the views, the big rooms. Two fireplaces. I mean WOW!

As we were wrapping up I remember standing on the deck and crying because I loved this home. Crying because I knew this was my house. I wanted it so bad. I felt it with every bone in my body. Just like you know when you choose your wedding dress. When you know, you know. It was no coincidence that we went to see this home. But $200K over our budget!

Well, if there is a will there's a way. We found a way to pull together the extra funds and put in an offer. If it's meant to be, it will be. The offer was accepted! We became homeowners.

Trust me, it's a process to purchase your first home, but it is possible. This made me think that if this is possible, everything and anything is possible. You just have to have the willpower to do it and move forward with it. I knew that if I could achieve this I could achieve anything I set my mind to.

See how I stated this: "Put your mind to"? Your mind is a very powerful thing. I am sure you have heard that before. This experience opened my eyes to many more possibilities and things I wanted to achieve.

236 Sea St
Weymouth, MA 02191

$1,050,000	8	4.5	4,373
Sold Price	Beds	Baths	Sq Ft

You have to let go of things and people that are holding you back to create the life you always wanted. As motivational speaker Bob Proctor says, "You can have anything you want. You just have to decide what you want and do everything it takes to get it. Get it. You have to know what you want to get it."

Where do you see yourself in life? What are the things you want to achieve? How would you envision your dream life? Your success?

You may want to purchase a property. You may want to fall in love and get married. You may see yourself traveling and having lots of money.

Now, ask yourself: What kind of property? What kind of partner or wedding would you like? Where would you like to travel? How much money? Million? Billion? Trillion? Think of the life you always wanted. Now write down what it is that you truly want. Focus on one thing. Write it in the present tense and with the feeling of having it already.

Now ask yourself, what actions are you willing to take to create your vision?

Write down anything that comes to mind. Let yourself brainstorm ideas.

 *Exercise*

Listen to this video. Near the end, there will be a challenge assigned to you. Make sure you have a pen and a piece of paper. Using a journal would be ideal. If you don't have a journal, purchase one so that you may use it throughout the rest of this book.

-3-

Eliminate Toxic Influences

Step 3: Eliminate Toxic Influences

A toxic influence can be a person, a place, or a behavior that can make us feel bad about ourselves and cause harm to our health, happiness, and well-being. They can also be relationships, drugs or alcohol, social media, self-image, etc. Toxic influences can often leave us feeling drained of mental and emotional strength. They don't bring out the best in us. Toxic influences have a negative effect on you and your life.

Finally, after 13 years of marriage, I was able to end my toxic marriage with my ex and filed a restraining order against him. A divorce was filed and I was finally free from this toxic relationship.

I had friends, but I was friends with women who gossiped about each other and made fun of each other instead of supporting each other. They wanted to be better than the next and were jealous of someone having better things than them.

Some friends distanced themselves from me when I filed for a restraining order. This made it easier for me to let go of them. God knows what He is doing when He removes certain people from your life when you can't. He creates space for better ones.

I now know to ignore what people think of me and my life. These people had a toxic influence on me, and I never felt their support to elevate and do what I truly wanted to do. One even told me that I should not write a book because everyone was writing a book!

As I eliminated my toxic relationship, the toxic friends removed themselves from me. They chose sides, and that's fine. This gave me the space to focus on myself and become a better person and focus on the positive aspects of myself and my life.

These people really did me the biggest favor because I never felt like I fit in with them. I had dreams and aspirations I wanted to achieve. I wanted to fulfill my purpose and I felt limited by these people and my surroundings.

I was elevating to a higher level in my life and God did everything to remove the old and replace it with the new.

"For I know the plans I have for you. Plans to prosper you and not harm you, plans to give you hope and a future"- Jeremiah 29:11.

I trusted in His plans for me. If I did not let go of things or people or even the place I resided, God did everything to remove me from those things. He knew I wanted to elevate my life.

Removing toxicity from your life is essential, especially toxic relationships. Remove people, places, and environments that do not serve you or help you grow.

Remember how I discussed willpower at the beginning of the book? Well, it takes a lot of willpower and thought to control and leave the toxicity and make changes in your life for the better.

Sometimes you really have to let go of everything and focus on yourself. You have to let go of what no longer serves you to go to the next level. Have time for yourself and your goals. Enjoy your time and use it wisely. You are what you invest in and surround yourself with.

Eliminate people who make you feel bad about yourself. This is the most important thing you can do above all things.

Start thinking positively about yourself and your situation, good or bad, because everything happens for a reason.

Start thinking positively about your life because you only have one.

Start thinking positively, especially about yourself, because no one can be you or believe in you but yourself.

Focus on the positives of everything. Even though you might be going through a tough time, trust me, it's for your own good, and there will be a positive outcome.

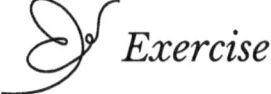 *Exercise*

Think about a current relationship you are in, whether it's with a friend, a boyfriend, or your spouse. Ask yourself seriously, is it healthy? Does it support you? Does it uplift you? Is there clear communication? Is there mental and emotional support? Is there? Is your environment providing a healthy status in your well-being? Does it bring out the best in you? Do you feel at peace?

It's so important to let go of toxic influences. Some other toxic traits can include:

- Toxic work environments that do not serve you.
- Toxic environments that you live in.
- Toxic relationships with people.
- A toxic relationship with money.
- The toxic influence of media, whether it's the news or social media.
- Toxins in the body.

You have to be ready for change. Now I want you to write down what you are trying to let go of and how it's not serving you.

Now I want you to write down what you want. I know this is a little bit repetitive but you have to repeat it. See it. Believe it. This is your life! If you do not believe in yourself who will?

Write down who you want to be and the life you want to live.

-4-

Invest in Yourself

Step 4: Invest in Yourself

What does it mean to invest in yourself?

I look at it this way: become the person you always wanted to be. Put in time, money, and energy into improving your current life. Start to walk, talk, act and present yourself like the person you always wanted to become, mentally and physically. Start to be or become that person. Invest time learning about this new person. Invest in a new mindset, new approaches to life, being in new environments. Invest in yourself to become the best version of yourself where you are on your way to fulfilling your dreams. It all starts with you.

After struggling with low self-esteem, low self-worth and not seeing my value, I felt pushed around by others. I never felt good enough, pretty enough, or worthy enough of good things happening to me. This was due to how I was brought up and the mindset that was in my subconscious. I was brought up that I did not need to be flashy and show off what I had, but now I know that this can be sharing your accomplishment with others. I was brought up not to dress in expensive clothes because it was seen as a waste of money, but this only left me with average motivation. I was brought up to work, work, and work and save money . . . for what? Wasn't I supposed to enjoy life and invest in things that can bring me more money?

The first thing I started to invest in was my mindset. Like I mentioned previously, I did this through meditation, affirmations, and motivational speakers. You are what you think, and what you think becomes your reality. I changed my thoughts of seeing myself reaching and living my dream life. I saw myself as a multi-millionaire. This changed my approach to things, which created the life I want to live and allowed me to reach more things in life.

I started to invest in my physical appearance. I made sure my hair always looked nice. I dressed really well, wearing my best outfits. I love dressing over the top and I love wearing what I want. I love to match. I love looking like a supermodel. I love to wear heels, whereas before I felt insecure because I was tall. Now I own my height and I love it!

I started to keep my nails looking nice. I did facials while taking a bath or watching my favorite shows. I started to eat healthier. I made a smoothie after a workout. I invested in my teeth and began having my teeth whitened. A beautiful smile says a lot about your hygiene.

I invested in laser hair removal. My bikini area looks better, which made me feel better and confident wearing a bikini doing photoshoots.

I invested my time at the gym. This helped me both mentally and physically.

I invested my time in learning. Reading books, googling almost everything, listening to Bob Proctor, and taking his seminars to better myself.

I invested in my mental health the most. I invested in learning a new way to speak, think, and the words I used and in which order. I would refer to myself as the person I knew I already was.

Reaching my goals drove me to becoming successful. Once I had reached my goal, it gave me more confidence to set another goal and reach it.

The more time I spent on things I want to accomplish, the closer I became to living my dream life. I rewarded myself. I rewarded myself with champagne, going out with the girls, or taking myself out shopping. Rewards are very important to celebrate the small steps you took to get to where you are going.

I invested in new speaking patterns, and had patience with myself when speaking and getting to know others. I was able to get resources that helped me in reaching my goals.

I invested a lot in developing my emotional intelligence, which gave me the capacity to be aware of, control, and express my emotions in handling a situation with another party. This created better relationships for me with men and women, and I allowed myself to be happy with myself for not overreaching, but responding.

After investing in myself, I felt more confident, more powerful, more of the person I always wanted to be. I felt free. I became a Queen with high standards and expectations that was able to say no to things that did not align with me. I was able to attract the things I always wanted. My dream town of Hingham that I currently live in. Best schools for my children to attend. I was able to attract wealth and new job opportunities.

I was able to have conversations and express what I wanted and needed to others. My new communications skills allowed me more opportunities to open doors and get me closer to my dreams, such as connecting with Green Heart Living Press, the company that published this book.

I was able to attract more money. More acting gigs. Higher paying jobs. People knew who I was because I knew who I was. I was taken more seriously professionally. I finally knew who I was and what I deserved, because of the time I invested in myself. I became the person I truly wanted to be. I was able to receive all the things I wanted and desired, and it all started by investing in myself first.

Start investing in yourself. What's the best way? Start taking responsibility for your life.

 *Exercise*

I want you to google "how to invest in yourself." Take notes in your journal on what you feel inspired by.

Write down the real version of you in the present tense like you are already this person. Start out with "I am . . ."

-5-

Know What You Want

Step 5: Know What You Want

To want something is a desired state of mind. It creates an attitude of possibilities and creates a release of dopamine, a neurotransmitter that helps us feel good and causes feelings of pleasure. Getting what you want can release those same pleasure chemicals, and our natural addiction to feeling good as we attain it.

First, you have to ask yourself what is it that you want?

Are you going to accept something that is less than what you want?

I wanted to get married at a young age. I did. I was married at the age of 21. I wanted a Gucci bag. I got it. I received my first expensive purse from my ex. I wanted to purchase a two-family home that was side by side. After finally stepping out of my comfort zone I was living in a mansion. I wanted to live in Higham, after my long, but very worthwhile journey, starting in South Boston, to Dorchester, to Quincy, to Weymouth I am now living in Hingham.

It's the attitude. The attitude of *I want it, I got it.*

I wanted to be a model for big brand names, and I am. Wella Hair brand, Moxy Hotel, and even sponsored by BEBE for a sunglasses ad. I wanted to be an actress. I am on my third movie, *The Collaboration,* and am filming my first HBO series *Julia.*

There have been times I settled. Settled for mediocre restaurants when I knew I was deserving of better. Settled for guys that were interested in me because I was excited about the attention. I settled for people treating me wrong because I was manipulated and thought this was normal. I settled for the wrong relationships because it was nice to have someone. I created future potential visions that never existed.

I settled for what could have been instead of what was.

After settling and ignoring my needs, I took those experiences as life lessons. I stopped being nice and blocked people that were not treating me the way I wanted to be treated. I know, blocking may be extreme, but it was a way I would cut them off from my energy. This is better than settling for someone who is wrong for you. I spent time alone and focused on myself and my wants, which really is another word for my goals. This always made me feel better and more productive knowing I was reaching what I wanted.

I knew what I wanted and had to start saying no to things that did not align with me. My friends were going out, but I began saying no, and felt at ease. I had to put my needs first because I knew what was right for me. When I did things that I wanted and got what I wanted, I would feel confident, happy, and in control of my life.

If I am in a relationship and I have communicated my wants and needs and they are not being met, I leave that relationship. Why would I settle for one less than I deserve? I would only get treated less than.

It's important to know what you want and never settle. When you settle you are being comfortable and comfortable does not get you anywhere.

If you want to be a real estate agent and make big money, start shifting to higher-end and expensive real estate markets. Want to become a model? Start submitting yourself to modeling agencies, investing in photoshoots, and thinking like you are already this person. You want to be a millionaire? Act like one and you will attract opportunities and knowledge for how to become one.

Know your worth. You are destined for greatness, so why would you settle? When you know your worth you never settle until you get what you want.

You have to know what you want and decide you will not stop until you get it. What is it that you want?

 *Activity*

Write down all the things that you want. A relationship. Tangible things. Vacations. Dreams.

Do not settle until you get them.

KNOW WHAT YOU
WANT, COMMIT TO IT,
AND LIVE IT.

-6-

Face Your Fears

Step 6: Face Your Fears

Facing your fears is a type of exposure that involves gradually and repeatedly going into feared situations until you feel less anxious. Facing your fears allows you to grow and move from where you are. Facing your fears helps you develop a growth mindset and become a person of action, change, and success.

It is normal to want to avoid the things you fear, however, on the other side of fear is success. The avoidance prevents you from learning that the things you fear are not as scary as you think. You come to know how many amazing things and opportunities there are with facing your fears.

For example, as a child, you had to face your fears of learning how to walk. Look at how determined you were. When you fell, what did you do? YOU GOT BACK UP! You faced your fears because you knew you really wanted to walk. You had determination, persistence, and motivation. There were many times you failed. In the end, it was all worth it. You are walking.

I will mention my divorce a few times in this book because it was a life-changing event and the biggest fear I had to overcome. I was married for 10 years and with this man for 13. We had been together since I was 20 years of age. I will not share too much detail, but it was an unhealthy relationship. There were the good times when our love was over the moon, but there was an unhealthy cycle where things would crash really tragically. I wanted out. Not only was I scared to get out because I was financially dependent on him, but I was also scared emotionally. I was attached.

When I thought about leaving, I was afraid. I was afraid I would lose my children because I had no income to support them. At my bible study, the Polish priest preached that divorce was not an option, which also made me feel fearful.

I felt stuck in my marriage like a prisoner.

After having some time to myself while recovering from my car accident and sleeping at my brother's house, I finally had the courage to stand up for myself, put all the fears aside and file for a restraining order and keep it. I had to face my fear of my new financial situation of starting out with no income. I had to face my fears of leaving everything behind and starting new all by myself. Once I faced my fears, my new life started.

Having DCF involved in our situation gave me many resources that helped me while being a single mother. I was able to apply for food stamps and government assistance of around $381 every two weeks. This helped me to provide needed essentials for myself and my two children. I felt ashamed. I was living in a mansion on government assistance. I was at my lowest, and I just felt that everyone was laughing at me, as punishment for filing a restraining order and leaving my ex-husband.

I also had many bills I was left to pay for which I used my credit cards cash advance to cover. I was experiencing a financial crisis that was incredibly tough. All I did was try my best. Even though I could not afford to take my children anywhere, I did my best to take them to the beach in the summer, on playdates, and to parks. In the winter we enjoyed the snow around us. I enjoyed and appreciated what I had, but deep down I was hurting. This was not me. I knew deep down I was a successful, independent, wealthy woman. I always told myself that the bad times were always temporary and that there would be a rainbow after the storm.

During this fresh detachment from my previous life, I took time to myself to learn and overcome fears such as my finances and relationships. I learned how to be on my own with the support of real friends that always supported me and were there for me, especially for my mental health, and supported my dreams.

My fears of finance started to diminish slowly as I was getting back on my feet. At this point, I now started to receive multiple sources of income because in my head I knew I was a multimillionaire. You have to start somewhere.

I was awarded child support and did DoorDash in the wintertime while the kids watched a movie in the car as I drove around. Liquor promos started to resurface after Covid-19. I booked my first movie role. I was making money. I faced my fear of finances. I faced my fear of divorce and I faced my fear of relationships by having a small supportive and trustworthy circle.

Now, I am grateful for all this happening to me, because I would not have faced my fears if I did not step into them. I would not have made it to where I am today: Successful and living my dream life.

When you face your fears, you step into success and growth where you become more confident, which inspires you to do more and become dedicated to accomplishing more things. Facing your fears is essential to thriving and succeeding in life.

 *Exercise*

The first thing I recommend doing is writing your top three fears.

1.

2.

3.

Now step out of your comfort zone and take action toward them. This is the hard part, but I promise you if you want to get over these fears you have to do something you have never done before.

Transform yourself. Develop a new mindset. A new belief system about yourself. Develop courage. Know that you can do it. Get where you want to be and not where someone else thinks you should be.

Once you step into one fear, and come out on the other side of it, your confidence and self-worth increase. Now you have the strength to step into your next fear. You push and you become stronger. Day after day you make progress and you build momentum. You now become stronger mentally and accelerate in self-development.

Now ask yourself, what action will you take first?

Take notes in your journal.

-7-

Manifest Everything

Step 7. Manifest Everything

Manifestation generally means using our thoughts, feelings, and beliefs to bring something to our physical reality. Seeing and believing like we already have it. This is why I stress it is important to have a new mindset because our thoughts are our creations. It's wanting something. Being someone. We produce a feeling, such as excitement, like we already have it. It's the frequency in which we bring ourselves to believe we already have it and we stay on this frequency to attract it. This goes together with the law of attraction.

You want it. Act like you already have it. You got it.

I definitely manifested my marriage, my divorce, being a young mom, my marital home, my dream town of Hingham, vacations, multiple sources of income, and much more that I currently have. These are the most important ones.

First, you have to appreciate everything you have to receive more.

With manifestation did come waiting. This waiting period was when God prepared me for what was coming. What lessons or experiences would I have encountered if I received everything I wanted at once? I had to get prepared for things I received, in God's timing or, in other words, divine timing.

I love telling the story about my divorce. I mean if this isn't God's perfect timing then I do not know what is. It is amazing to believe that I finally had the courage to stand up to my ex when we bought our first home. In no way did I even think about divorce when we bought our home. I mean we bought our first home! And this was in the midst of the Covid-19 pandemic in October 2020. It was exciting, but with a home came a lot of work and stress. The unhealthy cycle continued and I wanted out but did not know how.

In February of 2021, I was in a three-car accident. During this time, I stayed at my brother's house to recuperate and heal. This gave me time to heal myself and reprogram my mind. Thank God this accident happened. Seriously. This allowed me to start becoming the person I always dreamed of. With all this new knowledge and power I was able to stand up to my ex and file a restraining order and make progress toward the divorce. Now look at how this all happened. In God's perfect timing. House, accident, healing, divorce.

During the divorce stage, my ex sold the house and we were able to do an early withdrawal from the home's escrow, and BOOM, I had money to survive as a single mom. Imagine if we got a divorce when I was renting an apartment. God knows what he is doing. After the house sold, God leveled me up and moved me to the only place that accepted my application: Avalon at the Hingham Shipyard. At times I still cannot believe I live here.

I manifested living in this town. At the beginning of our house search, I had always written #1 for Hingham. I guess I had to leave the old things and people that no longer served me to allow my manifestations to come true. I never thought I would be living in a fancy place like the Hingham Shipyard. I manifested my vacation to Florida, and BOOM! I was flown to Ft. Lauderdale, Florida, first class, and stayed at the Ritz-Carlton. I manifested my luxury life when I ate at fancy restaurants, stayed only at five-star resorts, and traveled every month.

I am living my dream life being an actress, model, and author in Hingham. I started to attract everything and everyone I wanted. Beyond my expectations! I even manifested writing this book!

I believe I had to be a healed person to allow things to happen the way that they did, for me to get blessed like this. After I let go of the toxic things and people that were just holding me back, things were only getting better and better. I was prospering and attracting wealth, health, and abundance.

The way to start manifestation is through visualization, belief, and being ready to receive. With thoughts come actions, so make sure you take actions aligned with your thinking.

Visualize and be confident in your visualization. Have pictures. Draw them, cut them out of magazines, print them out from the internet and place them where you can see them often: on your mirror, your phone screensaver, or next to your bed.

Journal. Journaling allows you to physically see the words on paper and express your feelings while writing. Journaling is also a healing mechanism that allows you to see your faults and improve yourself. You are what you attract.

Speak your manifestations into existence.

For example: *I am so happy and grateful now that I am engaged and I have a 10-carat diamond on my ring finger. I am so happy and grateful I am a supermodel walking in Paris Fashion Week for Valentino, Chanel, Versace, and many more high-end design brands. I am so happy and grateful now that I am featured on the covers of the Sports Illustrated Swimsuit issue and Maxim magazine. I am so happy and grateful now that I am a multimillionaire and can retire by the age of 35.*

When you write down your manifestations, say them like you already have them in full detail and create a feeling when you speak about them.

Do not give up. Some manifestations take a while which may discourage you, but they are coming. You have to believe you are ready to receive them. Opportunities will come that require you to take them. Taking action and stepping out of your comfort zone will bring you closer. Remember you have to be your manifestation first.

Trust that every opportunity is a step closer to your dreams. Enjoy the journey. Things do not happen overnight. God will prepare you for these manifestations, so when the time is right He will make it happen. When the time finally comes you will not believe how good it gets.

Be grateful for what you have so you can attract more. Remember your current situation does not define you, but you do have to be grateful for it. This is a lesson, an experience, a test to see if you are ready for your next abundance because you have to fully develop into the person who is ready to have them. Always stay positive and think positively.

The big part about manifestations is that you have to let go of the old you, the old life, including friends, relationships, and environments, to attract better and welcome the new. Trust me, things will get hard, and stress and anxiety will happen, but in the end, you just have to believe and have faith that your manifestations will come true.

 *Activity*

This activity is going to be fun for you.

Draw, print, save. Do what you have to to see your manifestations. With every manifestation, write down how you would feel if you already had it. Where you would be, what you would be wearing. Be specific and detailed.

Make any physical visual manifestation to be somewhere you know. The more you see it the more you want it, the more you will get it. Remember to talk about your manifestations like you already have them. Create the feeling associated with them. The more relaxed you are about your manifestations, the faster they come.

August 13, 2021

Manifested Trip
to Florida

June 22, 2022

The Ritz in Florida

-8-

Develop
a Routine

Step 8: Develop a Routine

A routine is a sequence of actions followed regularly. It is the practice of regularly doing things in a fixed order. Develop a routine. A healthy routine. A new routine. The old one brought you to where you are, but to move forward you need to make and adapt to new changes. You have to start with a new routine for the new you and be grateful for the old routine that brought you here.

Remember the new you is the new routine. Successful. Driven. Wanting change. New routine, new you. Impactful. Remember: *New Routine, New You.* Yes. I will repeat this many times to get this embedded into your subconscious. *New Routine, New You.* Routine with discipline. Routine with purpose. Routine for change. New changes. Successful changes will get you closer to your dreams. *New Routine, New You.*

In the past, I never really had a routine. It was difficult because I had two small children under my supervision and constantly needed to take care of them. Even while married, I felt like a single mom; helpless, angry, frustrated, and alone. The only part of my routine I remember from that time was going out running when my ex arrived home early. I had to run for my mental and physical health.

As I came across having more time for myself, due to the parenting agreement made by the judge, I was able to focus more on myself and things to do to make myself into a better person. Mental health became a priority.

I started out with meditation first thing in the morning. Now, I meditate on everything. I wake up at six am and look for a meditation that will help me to set my day. I search on YouTube for videos such as "guided meditation for a good day", "guided meditation for creativity and success", "guided meditation for confidence", or "guided meditation for a new beginning."

Meditation has helped me set the tone for the day and has helped me to reprogram my subconscious to create positive results.

While I was still sleeping at my brother's house during my recovery from my car accident, every morning I would drive to my marital home to take care of my kids. Do you know what I would do while driving? I would listen to motivational speakers. Damn, they are raw! They speak facts, and truly inspire and motivate you. They gave me a burst of energy in the morning. They did not care if I failed, but encouraged me to get the hell up again because why would you want to stop in hell!? There were no excuses for giving up. They were intense.

As I wrapped up my physical therapy, I continued my recovery and signed up for the gym. I am and always have been in good physical shape because I am an active person, but a gym provides more than that. I signed up for Lifetime Fitness at Westwood, Massachusetts. This place changed my whole perspective of a regular gym. It's like a spa. This gym not only motivated me to work on my body, but also my mind, body, and soul. I loved the incredible classes from Gluteus Maxout to hot yoga. From outdoor pools to indoor saunas and steam rooms. For me, this was a whole transformation that impacted my life. I not only got a workout in, but also met some incredible, motivated, successful, and supportive friends. We all have one goal: to become better each day. It all starts with a healthy mental and physical state.

Overall, the three new routines that helped me were:

1. Meditation

2. Motivational speakers

3. Gym (change of lifestyle)

With this new routine, I gave time to myself. This was the most important and healthiest thing I could have done for myself. It helped me become the best version of myself.

With meditation, I reprogrammed my subconscious mind with new beliefs. Motivational speakers helped me move toward where I wanted to be in life. The gym allowed me to release feel-good endorphins and other natural brain chemicals that enhanced my sense of well-being.

 *Exercise*

Find a guided meditation on YouTube. It can be anything you want to meditate on. Choose one that is at least 10 minutes long. Listen to it. After listening to it go back, and while listening again take notes in your journal. Go ahead . . .

Every day you listen to a meditation, try to go back after, and take notes. This is a visual way to program as well. You are reprogramming yourself in two ways: 1) listening, where it is being implemented in your subconscious, and 2) taking notes as a visual to confirm the new knowledge.

Next, listen to motivational videos. Try listening while you commute to work, go to a friend's house, or drive long distances. Let this become your new routine. Trust me, as you are investing your time, your mind and your lifestyle will change. Change is growth and the only way to grow is to change. This will build courage, confidence, and self-worth, and prepare you for your successful, dream life.

Lastly, google gyms around you. When I moved to Hingham Shipyard I had a gym at my site so I canceled my membership with Lifetime, but I miss it so much every day. I would go to my gym for the environment, put on a YouTube video, put in my ear pods, and start working out. You can also exercise in the comfort of your own home. You have to push yourself. BOOM. Easy as 1, 2, 3. The best part of exercising with YouTube videos is that you can do it at whatever time works for you, you do not have to wait or rush to catch a certain class. Stay motivated and disciplined.

-9-

Engage in Self-Care

Step 9: Engage in Self-Care

Self-care is the practice of taking action to preserve or improve one's own health. This is about living healthy, whether it's eating better, sleeping better, surrounding yourself with better people, or most importantly, enjoying things you like to do. This will also help you stay true to you and your authentic self. Self-care is all about improving and becoming a better version of yourself. It's pretty simple—you just enjoy being the real you!

Taking care of two small children simultaneously at home, being a good wife, and helping my ex with the success of his business, I did not have time for self-care, nor did I know what it was. I noticed the drain it was on me. I was making sure everyone was taken care of first instead of me.

Eating healthy was always a priority in my household, but sleeping . . . that's another story. I was constantly sleep deprived. From breastfeeding to changing diapers at night to comforting my children when they had a bad dream, I was always on my toes. I also, somehow, had to manage to have energy during the day to take care of my boys. I could definitely feel it took a toll on me in my everyday life and mental health. I was not myself.

I had very limited time to do what I liked to do. When I did try to do what I enjoyed, like take a bath, I heard my children and my ex through the door. This was not relaxing. I danced with the kids at home and colored with them to allow me to enjoy the things I liked and things that brought me peace, even though my boys liked to color together with me on one page. Yup, this summarizes it. I never had any alone time.

Now with joint custody, and having a schedule of who has time with the children, I now have alone time where I can focus on my self-care to become better for me so I can be better for my children.

My self-care consists of doing things alone that I enjoy. I enjoy going to the gym by myself where I can do any exercise I want. I love enjoying my time in the sauna and jacuzzi to refresh, let go of toxins, and better myself physically and mentally.

Now I take a nice long bath at home without the interruptions of anyone needing me. Hot water makes me calm and relaxed. Sometimes I add some candles, flowers, or a glass of champagne to celebrate myself and feel fancy. I love to play positive spa music with no words while I bathe. Just lay there in peace. In warmth. Alone. Enjoying my own presence. Enjoying my time for myself and doing things that make me feel good, relaxed, and at peace.

I also enjoy sunbathing. The beams of the sun feel so good. So relaxing. So warm. I will either do this in the backyard or lay out on the beach where I can listen to the beautiful and calming sounds of waves. There is something about the ocean that calms me down and makes me feel so free.

From time to time I will splurge on getting my nails and hair done and go shopping. I will get facials done, or do them myself while I indulge myself by watching my favorite shows *The Bachelorette* or *The Bachelor.* I cater to my appearance more and finally feel comfortable dressing how I always wanted to: extra.

I enjoy dressing up wherever I go. Looking good makes me feel good, and wearing what I want without caring what people's opinion of me is, makes me feel even better. I finally have the confidence to dress up as I always wanted to and I enjoy wearing my best outfits and heels. Why save them for a special occasion? Every day is a special occasion! I am the special occasion.

Therapy is also self-care. I have done three years of therapy and am still seeing my psychiatrist to continue being mentally healthy. I remember my first time seeing my psychiatrist. I thought there was something wrong with me. I cried my first time going. It was so hard and emotional.

I am so grateful I went. I started to tell my story and I was diagnosed with PTSD. I was prescribed medication, which I still take. As I am writing this I am sobbing tears of joy. I am so grateful for the mental help I received when I needed it the most.

It all starts with your mental health. If there is someone that does not support your mental health, please get rid of them. You will see how much relief you get.

Things I accomplished with my self-care: a better me, a healthier me, a more stable me. I was able to do things that helped me live well and improve both my physical and mental health. I manage stress better and have more energy for activities that I enjoy by myself and with my boys.

 *Exercise*

Self-care is the time you take care of yourself and your health. I want you to write down in your journal how you can take care of yourself. What does self-care look like for you?

Remember you have to take time for yourself. Get to know yourself. Seek help if needed. This is time for you. To be healthy, you need to have self-care days focused on you. This is a time to appreciate yourself. If you are ok with being by yourself then you can make better decisions and feel more in control of your own life. You have to enjoy being yourself, and this is a time to become the best version of yourself.

-10-

Practice Self-Love

Step 10: Practice Self-Love

Self-love is one of the most important things you need to learn about. This is a way you focus on yourself, your well-being, and your own happiness. Self-love means taking care of your own needs and not sacrificing your well-being to please others. Seeing your worth and value and your positive qualities. The highest form of self-love is taking action toward these goals.

Growing up, I did not have much self-love because of my past trauma. I was a failure at relationships with guys and girls. I did everything for people and I did not feel my worth or value because I valued others' opinions of me. Hanging with the wrong crowd and being a people pleaser allowed me to feel unworthy. I was a people pleaser and put others' needs before mine because I thought this would make them like me more. I ignored my happiness to fulfill theirs. I ignored the things I wanted to do that made me happy. Instead, I did things that my friends wanted to do to make *them* happy. I ignored my needs and wants to be there for my friends because, in the end, I thought they would be there for me.

I did not know how to say no, and with this, I lost my self-love. Giving people the benefit of the doubt to partake in the activities they wanted to do resulted in a lot of trauma and rejection of myself.

I compared myself to others but never wanted to be them. I always thought about how they deserved that man, or that bracelet, or that vacation, and I did not. I worried about what others thought about me having to file for divorce. A perfect couple getting a divorce. Everything looks beautiful on the outside.

I was constantly criticized for my mistakes, especially by the people closest to me. If I did not do something that others wanted they would blame the outcome on me.

Being criticized for mistakes took a toll on my mental health. I did not know how to make decisions on my own because I felt like they were always wrong. I fully doubted everything I did. I did not believe in myself or my decisions. The void of not having support or anyone to confide in took a toll.

Through my self-healing time, I learned about and practiced self-love. This made me realize I had to put myself first to be happy. The more I did for myself the more freeing and happy I was. This made me enjoy the things I loved to do without caring if anyone wanted to join me or not. Walks were always something I enjoyed, and having people around me not want to partake was fine. I did what made me feel happy and went on that walk alone, in peace.

Having to make decisions in my best interest and for my well-being, I started not attending many events and outings my friends were having. At that time I did not want to put myself in those environments. I had other plans for myself and used that time for my well-being. This allowed me to grow, become more confident and make healthier decisions. Most importantly, I was able to say no, set up boundaries, and walk away from all the toxicity in my life that no longer served me. I was able to be alone, focus on my well-being by going to the gym, take a month off from drinking, focus on my goals, and do what Angelika wanted to do.

Through my self-love journey, I was able to see my worth. My self-esteem rose tremendously. I started to think really positively about myself. With this, I started to believe in myself and my dreams. I became confident in making decisions for myself and not relying on others' acceptance of me. With this, I flourished in my life—becoming my most healthy, peaceful, happy, and loving self.

My advice: Start loving yourself first before you try to love others. Self-love allows you to get to know yourself better. Once you focus on yourself, you will learn how to love yourself. Once you learn to love yourself, you will be happy and confident in yourself. You will no longer put yourself in situations you do not want to. Once you love yourself, you will realize your worth and what you deserve, and will not allow others to treat you any other way.

Exercise

If you have been putting other people first for a long time, sometimes it can take some time to remember what things you enjoy.

Here are examples of what makes me happy:

1. Hot coffee in the morning

2. Talking to people

3. Helping others

4. Complimenting others

5. Spending time with my kids

6. Shopping

7. Being outdoors

8. Dancing

9. Listening to music

10. Being alone

Write things that make you happy:

1.

2.

3.

4.

5.

6.

7.

8.

9.

10.

Examples of positive qualities about myself:

1. Kind

2. Compassionate

3. Loving

4. Loyal

5. Trustworthy

6. Secure

7. Confident

8. Wise

9. Passionate

10. Ambitious

Write positive qualities about yourself:

1.

2.

3.

4.

5.

6.

7.

8.

9.

10.

Remember to love yourself just the way you are because God made you perfect in His eyes.

-11-

Control Your Thoughts

Step 11: Control Your Thoughts

Controlling your thoughts will influence the way you live your life. Your thoughts affect your perception, and therefore, your interpretation of your reality. Once you have control over your mind, you have control of your life. When you control your thoughts you have the ability to control unpleasant or unwanted intrusive thoughts. Intrusive thoughts are often triggered by stress or anxiety, as well as by recurring and unwanted past experiences. As humans, we are able to control only a tiny part of our conscious thoughts. The majority of our thinking efforts are subconscious. This is why it is so important to reprogram your subconscious.

Last night I could not sleep. I was in my head thinking about how to write a story about thoughts. I thought that if I slept on it I would wake up with great ideas, but I couldn't sleep. I woke up around 1:26 am, and I thought I would start writing the first thing that popped into my mind. I wrote about my dream. Then I thought, *what does my dream have to do with my thoughts? It actually has to do with your subconscious mind.*

I was thinking, overthinking, and observing. I was having conversations in my head with people. I was thinking about what I wish I had said to them when I was in their presence. This is why I realized that it is important to communicate what you are thinking in the present moment.

If I did not express what I was thinking I would create scenarios in my head that included people and places and create this whole story of what would happen, stress myself out and create anxiety in my body, experience a breakdown, and cry. Eventually, I would realize that I was thinking about something that hadn't happened yet and I was going all crazy about it! It is so important for me to control my thoughts and bring myself to the present moment and to remember I create my reality in the present moment.

When I experience intrusive or negative thoughts, it feels like I have a battle in my mind. First, because I don't know the outcome. Second, because I am creating an outcome in my mind and stressing about something that hasn't happened yet. Third, because I have experienced a result of this thought in the past, and I was naturally programmed to have the same negative thinking patterns.

This is how I started to change my life.

I was sitting in my place alone and thinking, *I am sad, I am alone, and bored.* These are negative thoughts. I tried to think the opposite of these, telling my brain: *I am happy, because being alone is better than being in an unhealthy relationship, and that I am at peace. This alone time allows me to focus on my goals. I am not bored because I am bringing my thoughts into action.*

My thoughts: *Write this book.* I started typing.

My thoughts: *Go to the gym.* I plan on a time when I can commit to working out.

My thoughts: *Get a divorce. Buy a house. Read a book.* These are all thoughts that I put into action and that created my reality.

When I put in action, my thoughts get things accomplished. When I get things accomplished, I feel good. When I feel good, I can do more. When I can do more I get closer to my dream life or the success I want to reach. I change my negative thinking and substitute it with positive thinking and action to help me create in the present moment.

After the negative experiences, trauma, and fear, I started to change my mindset and control my thoughts. Every time a negative thought would enter my mind I would observe it. I would acknowledge it and get curious: *Why was I thinking like this? Why was I feeling like this? What is it telling me?* Then I would try to create a positive thought in response. Sometimes I would have a whole conversation in my head and that's when I would lean on meditation or refocus myself on the present moment. If I got into my head too much I would meditate or talk it out with friends.

Many of our thoughts are brought to us through the influence of other people or by our past experiences. You can refer to it as brainwashing or manipulation. This is because someone else gave you an idea and you thought about it, allowing it to affect you without the proper ideology. Past experiences allow us to also have deep subconscious thoughts. For example, when someone cheats on you, you have a thought that the next person will cheat on you too. Once you reprogram this thought, that is when thought control takes place.

Taking control of your thoughts in a more positive way creates a better life. I know unexpected things will happen, but if you think positively about them you look at things from a whole different perspective. Your thoughts create your reality so please be careful about what you think about. Your positive thinking will allow you to create the life you always dreamed of.

Here are some ways you can control your thoughts:

- Mediation
- Positive affirmation self-talk
- Take a pause out of your life to calm your busy thoughts and do something for you
- Avoid things that may cause negative thoughts, like scrolling through social media
- Distract yourself
- Question your thoughts
- Readjust your life goals
- Develop your self-esteem and confidence
- Focus on the present moment only
- Exercise
- Recreate the story in your head

 *Activity*

When you have any thoughts that pop up into your head, ask yourself:

Why am I thinking this?

How can I change this thought?

What positive outcome can I create from this?

-12-

Release the Trauma

12. Release the Trauma

We all have a little trauma stored in our system. This may be associated with a particular memory, often on the subconscious level. This is why I stress that it is so important to program a new subconscious way of thinking. In order to let go you have to release what's holding you back, the old ways of thinking or the past actions that caused you trauma. I know this might not be easy, but it is doable.

Carrying your trauma creates a blockage for your blessing, opportunities, and abundance. For me, it all started with not having a relationship with my parents. Seeing my mother abused, I allowed that in my marriage and past relationships. It seemed normal at the time. Having "fake" friends who maneuvered me through life and manipulated me influenced some of the bad life decisions I made for myself. This brought my confidence, self-esteem, and self-worth down. I held onto my emotions and did not express my feelings, needs, and wants because they were constantly being ignored. Since I held onto my emotions and feelings because I did not know how to express them verbally, I attracted the same relationships where the only communication was through abuse because there was no communication or it wasn't handled properly. I felt ignored and the abuse continued.

I was scared of abandonment and became a people pleaser. I wanted people to like me and not leave me, even if this included me ignoring my truth and lying to people to allow them to hear what they wanted.

The abandonment started with my family as I was the youngest child out of five. I would be excluded from many outings and events because I was too young. Then my older siblings started to get into relationships and I felt alone. The ending of relationships made me feel fragile and not good enough.

In the end, all I wanted was to be loved by someone. I would automatically respond to new relationships with excitement and trust too fast. With guys, I become clingy which got me nowhere because I did not know my worth, and with girls, I felt a lot of competition and not worthy enough because they would always get hit on and not me.

You may wonder how I managed all of this stored-up trauma that caused me to have emotional distress and aggressive outbursts like a child. I had childhood trauma, and lots of it, which affected my decisions, actions, and behavior into adolescence.

Therapy has helped me magnificently. I have enjoyed opening up to a professional and sharing my life. Having her listen and support me allowed me to see life differently. Therapy has allowed me to resurface things from my past, make connections to them with my present life, accept them, and make peace with them. This helped me set up a better road ahead.

Journaling also helped me a lot. I would write things down that I could not share with anyone, because of trust issues. I released my trauma on paper. I took notes in my journal on the new things I was taught. New behaviors, new approaches, and new outcomes.

I prayed for God to give me strength and get me through my suffering. I know He was always there to listen. It was a great way to talk out loud. Sometimes when you talk out loud and hear yourself it's different. I read the bible and applied it to my life, as well as attended church regularly every Sunday as Jesus is my savior.

I let go of friends that were not good for me. I learned that some friendships are here to serve their purpose and teach me a lesson. That some friends were not meant to be in my life forever. I realized that not everyone has the same life goals as me and not everyone is meant to be a part of my life long-term. Some relationships can be temporary and that's ok. Some can be for a lifetime if it's the type of friend that supports you and your mental health.

I meditated on anything that released my trauma and educated myself on it. I had to understand what I was going through and why, research it, and find ways to heal from it. Meditation was healing, and educating myself allowed me to become more powerful in the things I was lacking.

The only way I was able to heal and recover from my trauma was by learning about it, addressing it, and releasing it. Releasing my trauma allowed me to release my past and make room for the beautiful future that is in store for me. This allowed me to let go of old unhealthy patterns, thoughts, and actions and replace this with new traits and better habits, and more positive outcomes. I am a strong person because of my past experience. I would not be where I am if it wasn't for my past events. So I am grateful for what has happened and have chosen to get past it and move on.

I recommend you release your trauma. Talk to someone, write it down, research it, find new approaches, but do accept it. Your trauma brought you here today, but you do not need to keep letting it affect you.

 *Activity*

Write down in your journal what trauma you have experienced in your life.

Research this trauma.

What are some ways that you can release this trauma?

-13-

Seek God
Not Revenge

13. Seek God Not Revenge

Revenge is the action of inflicting hurt or harm on someone for wrongs suffered at their hands. An opportunity to retaliate. A payback. A punishment to harm someone for what they have done to you. Revenge is wanted when a person does you wrong, you seek revenge and do wrong to them as well. Revenge is retaliation for hurting people.

Is it worth it? Absolutely not.

To me, revenge is for weak, small-minded people that have nothing better to do with their lives. Does it work? Probably, in the short run, but in the end, it backfires. Revenge is only sought by the weak. They feel inferior and are trying to find a way to feel superior to others who did them wrong.

In my life, I have had to get past the damage that has been thrown at me. I focused on taking good care of my children and living my best life. I have allowed God to fight my battles. Instead of seeking revenge on people that have done me wrong in my life, I have continued to get my life on track. If I tried to seek revenge it would only mean that they still have power over me.

Instead of wasting my time seeking revenge, I focused on bettering myself. This is the best thing I could have done. I came to know the real me, what I deserve, and how I should be treated. I stood up for myself. I finally had a voice.

I would recommend focusing all your time and energy on yourself and not plotting revenge on every person that did you wrong. In the end, success tastes better than revenge. Time wasted cannot be retrieved, so use your time wisely. When you try to get revenge it only means that that person still has power over you, so move on and do not allow them to take over your energy, space, or feelings.

Focus on your goals. Know that God is working in your favor and will serve justice on your behalf. Revenge is only for the weak and you my friend are strong for not lowering yourself to those standards. Just let go and do you. That's my best advice. Do not get revenge or get even, just do you. Because your being successful will be the best revenge ever.

 *Exercise*

Write everyone's name on a paper that you feel has caused you suffering. Say, "I forgive you." Pray for them. Burn the paper and allow God to take over.

-14-

Forgive Yourself and Others

Step 14. Forgive Yourself and Others

Forgiveness allows you to find peace within yourself. Forgiveness is important to the healing process since it allows you to let go of the anger, guilt, shame, sadness, and any other feelings you may be experiencing from your past. Forgiving yourself is allowing you to bring peace to your life, mind, and your heart. Forgiving yourself and others for all the mistakes that were done allows you to let go of your trauma, negativity, and anything that is holding you back from moving forward. It allows you to let go of resentment and move forward and live your best life.

Have you ever been in a relationship where you were being honest but the other person wasn't? Have you ever been with someone who had a mask on? I have. As things progressed I started to like him more—because the mask was on. He was not only giving me attention but also coming to see me regularly. He pursued me and I allowed him to take the lead in our relationship. Not only was I in love with him, I thought we were destined to be together, and this was finally our chance.

Then things took a turn. He would say negative things about my breasts or tell me I should get my breasts done. I am a woman that is completely comfortable with my body and I replied by saying, "I love them." When I asked him if we were on the same page he would reply, "Stop being so insecure." I am a very secure person, and I am very secure in my relationships. It was a reflection of his own insecurities.

I found myself being love-bombed, manipulated, gaslighted, and settling for breadcrumbs. I didn't even know what those words were at the time—I learned them later. It's like I saw this person for who he truly was but still managed to ignore the truth. There were red flags, as red as fire, but I ignored them.

Why was this happening? Because I created in my mind the idea that this was my dream man. My dream man, though, would never have done things like this. He was actually a devil in disguise.

While seeing this masked man I ended up losing 10 pounds, but I had no idea why. Later I realized it was because my body was rejecting this person. My body was trying to tell me that this person was toxic. As he looked at my Instagram stories I would think he was interested, but his communication with me became distant. When he interacted with my posts it gave me a dopamine hit. It was crazy how my brain reacted. I have never felt like this before, especially mentally. As I tried to reach out to him to tell him I wanted to see him and spend time with him, I was constantly let down or ignored.

Thank God for people that create meditations because this was my lifesaver while I was mentally distraught in this relationship.

After a while, he started to ghost me. Why was he doing this when he was the one that wanted me? I really thought what he and I had was real because for years I somehow felt energetically connected to him. I figured out that he found someone else. My heart was broken and so were all the promises he made to me. I never experienced anything like this, so I did not know how to react and what to do. I was never in this position before where I experienced so much pain mentally and my body changed physically. I am grateful now he left and I chose to forgive myself for being a part of this relationship.

In my life, I've had many other opportunities to practice forgiveness. I'm sure you have too. How did I overcome all of this? I forgave myself. I forgave myself for my past. I forgave myself for the way I allowed people to mishandle me. I forgave my actions. In my heart, I forgave the people who hurt me the most. I forgave them and tried to understand why they hurt me: because hurt people hurt people.

Forgiving allows you to let go of the feelings and emotions associated with what went wrong. Forgiving others is a closure you give yourself that they might not give you. It does not mean a person will apologize to you or give you closure, this means that you are willing to forgive and walk away for how they mistreated you. Forgiving others allows you to move forward and detach yourself from the feelings and emotions you have for that person. Walking away is the biggest sign of self-love. This allows you to let go and gives you peace to live your life.

If you want to forgive someone or yourself I would recommend praying and accepting what has happened. Acknowledge your feelings of bitterness or betrayal. Allow yourself time to grieve, and leave the past in the past. Try to understand why the person did what he or she did. I would also suggest listening to meditations on forgiveness as well as researching strategies on how to forgive.

Exercise

I want you to finish each sentence:

I forgive myself for _____

I forgive you for _____

I am sorry for _____

I forgive you for _____

I forgive myself for _____

I am sorry for _____

I forgive you for _____

I forgive myself for _____

I am sorry for _____

Forgiveness takes time. Healing takes time. Remember things do not happen overnight. This is your journey to forgive, let go, and allow. Allow yourself to become the best version of yourself. It took me a full year to forgive some people. There is no timeline and do not put pressure on yourself.

-15-

Communicate Your Affirmations

Step 15. Communicate Your Affirmations

Affirmations are positive assertions about yourself and your life. They are confirmations of what you truly can become or who you truly are. Hearing affirmations and saying affirmations helps to reprogram your subconscious to think highly of yourself. They reprogram your thinking about yourself, helping you to believe in yourself and reach your highest potential. They affirm everything you want to become and have. The phrases or words become powerfully embedded in your mind as a new way of thinking and viewing yourself as your highest self.

Before affirmations, I doubted myself and the results of my life highly. I doubted the decisions I made and asked others for advice constantly. I did not feel like I could make my own choices because every time I made a decision I felt like it was wrong and always second-guessed it. I would engage in others' negative talk of me, of how I was stupid and how I should listen to them. Again, I was a people pleaser so I made many of my decisions based on what others wanted for me.

I never felt pretty or good enough. I am this beautiful woman on the exterior, but I never felt it on the interior. My height affected my confidence when I was growing up. I was very self-conscious. I remember one time I went out clubbing, I felt like I looked amazing. I was walking with the confidence of wearing high heels. These two guys passed by me and one said to the other, "Don't talk to her, that is a man." Damn, did that hurt. I was self-conscious about my height.

Now I see the value in my height and my beautiful long legs. Being tall and slim, I have done amazing modeling for huge brands like Matrix L'Oreal which was my first hair modeling gig. They even paid for my hotel stay.

When I did these jobs it felt unreal, so I did not appreciate these bookings as much as I see them today. I mean my first hair booking was L'Oreal! Getting paid well, hotel stay included, free products to take home, and an amazing staff that taught me my first runway walk. Can I also say my hair looked beyond amazing?

I had a hard time accepting that this was my reality because I pictured modeling differently. I could not believe that I was actually chosen and booked for modeling roles.

As I continued to expand my modeling career, I was rejected from many castings as well. I always wanted to know why I was not chosen for certain jobs, and not knowing made me dissect myself and my appearance even more. What did this girl have that I did not? It did not help that my significant other would say, "Oh, you're a model, where is all this money?" This made me pursue modeling even more, but the more jobs I booked I was still not getting paid enough to someone else's standards.

Affirmations changed my life and the way I saw myself. They made me believe who I really was and released all the negative thoughts, doubts, and beliefs I had about myself that were embedded in my subconscious through verbal abuse. Affirmations replenished my self-worth.

I realized that I was a beautiful person inside and out and that not everyone deserves to have me. Through affirmations, I acknowledged my value and my worth. My standards even went up more. I began thinking, *Yeah, if you want to date me you have to be rich, treat me well, be secure with yourself, and spoil me.* I finally knew who I was and I knew what I was worthy of.

All the rejections of not being booked for certain jobs only helped me prepare for what was really meant for me. Rejection only brought me closer to my dreams. Rejection is God's protection and God always has a better path for us.

Through affirmations, I started to look at things and outcomes more positively even when they were not the ones I wanted. I learned a few things along the way.

First, I learned not to rush good things. Yes, I rushed into relationships, both with guys and girlfriends. They backfired. It was not what I wanted, but it was what I was used to. I started to use affirmations such as "I am patient", "I allow things to happen", and "I can say no."

The second thing I learned was that there is a time for everything, everyone, and every place. I would say to myself: "I am where I am meant to be." This took a lot of anxiety away. If it's meant to be it will be. There is a reason behind everything you do, every person you meet, and every place you go. You have to use these experiences, even if they were bad, as opportunities and lessons to help you escalate to the next level of your life.

Third, failures are only lessons that will show us a different path to our desired outcome. So, yes, it's ok to fail as long as you get back up. Affirmations allowed me to believe I was worthy of all my dreams and desires which kept me going. I was able to believe in myself and the things that I am truly made for. No matter what happened, I came this far and I could not give up. Knowing I had a final destination kept me going and the affirmations kept me pushing.

I always started with "I" and spoke in the present tense like I was already this person and had the things I wanted. With believing I was creating, and was able to live my dream life. *I fly first class. I am in a healthy, loving relationship. I have supportive friendships. I am confident in myself and the decisions I make. I am living in my dream town of Hingham. I am so happy and grateful for the money that I receive in increasing quantities through multiple sources on a continuous basis. I am healthy. I am rich. I am successful. I am beautiful. I stay at the best hotels. I travel on vacations. I have written a best-selling book. I am a supermodel and Oscar-winning actress. I am living my best life. I am living my dream life. And I am literally living the life that I affirmed.*

I recommend you listen to affirmations on TikTok or YouTube and write them down and use affirmations during your meditation. Once a feeling is created in you, you start to believe them.

Listen to affirmations almost every single day. The best time is before you go to sleep so they will be embedded in your subconscious and be programmed as a new version you see yourself as. You are basically affirming everything you already are, but listening to them makes you believe even more and will help you get to where you want to be.

There are affirmations for certain topics:

Affirmations for confidence

Affirmations for self-love

Affirmations for money/wealth

Affirmations for health

Affirmations for becoming famous

Affirmations for success

You think of it. Affirm it.

 *Exercise*

Focus on something that you really want and who you really are and write it in the present tense like you already have it or that you already are this person.

I am _____

I am _____

I am _____

I am _____

Life changing.

-16-

Put Yourself First

Step 16 - Put Yourself First

Take into account your own needs and feelings as well as that of others, but do what's best for you. It's as easy as it sounds. Put yourself first. It's ok to put yourself first without feeling guilty. It's important to do so because nobody else is going to do that for you. If you prioritize yourself you pour into your own cup first so it overflows. Then you can pour into someone else.

When I prioritize myself, my wants, and my needs, I feel happy, successful, and at ease. I feel accomplished. I feel good. When I used to put other people's needs before mine, it messed with my self-esteem, my worth, and my happiness. This created a lot of anxiety for me. I was a people pleaser.

I ignored my needs in order to be there for someone else. I set aside my time at the gym to be with a guy. I put aside my goals to travel with my man. I did not know how to say no to my friends when they wanted to come over. I was neglecting myself and my needs for someone else. I was losing myself for someone else. My energy was drained and I took my anger and frustration out on people close to me. I was even ignoring my mental health to be there for others. Well, no more of that! I learned about putting myself first.

I took space for myself. I needed alone time and to just be away from everyone's needs. Alone time allowed me to rejuvenate my mind, peace, and happiness. It allowed me to prioritize what I enjoy. Being alone allowed me to watch my favorite shows or movies without interruption. It allowed me to write this book. Alone time allowed me to go to the gym. Now, I know alone time allows me to re-focus on myself. This feels satisfying to my own needs. I want to fulfill my own needs so I can be calm and happy because no one else can do this for me but myself.

Every morning I pray and meditate before I start my day. It's a way I take care of my mind, body, and soul before I can be there for someone. I go to the gym first before I meet up and hang out with friends.

I go to the grocery store to make sure I have everything I need instead of rushing to go out with my friends and then coming home and complaining that I don't have the groceries I needed to purchase. I clean my house before I go out anywhere because I love coming home to a clean space. Most importantly, I made time work for me. I know there is respect in time and having reservations, but I need to put myself first in getting ready to make sure I look my best because I want to feel my best.

I learned to say no when I did not want to go out. No to parties. No to people's time with me. I started to say no to things I did not enjoy or did not want to do. This felt great because it eased my anxiety about being pressured to do something or go somewhere I did not want to. This felt great because I was listening to myself and what I wanted. By saying no I was developing healthy boundaries. By having healthy boundaries I respected myself even more and felt much better about my decisions for myself.

Prioritizing myself gave me power over my life. The more I did for myself the more I felt accomplished. The more I did for myself the more I could help others. Prioritizing myself allowed me to reach higher goals that led me to my dreams.

If you constantly put other people and the things they want to do before the things you want to do, you slack in your own life. This may hold you back from achieving what you want. It could affect your physical and mental health. Sometimes, you may choose to set boundaries and distance yourself from certain things, people, and places so that you can prioritize your needs in order to be successful. It's a worthy investment.

 *Activity*

Below are a series of 10 questions with a yes or no answer. Please answer as honestly as you can. This is to help you understand you.

1. You initially have plans with your girlfriends and your crush asks you to hang out with you this day because this is his/her only available day. Do you cancel the plans with your girlfriends?

YES   NO

2. You just finished work and you are tired. Your friend asks you to come over. She needs support because she just broke up with their significant other. Do you go over?

YES   NO

3. Your friend asks you to do laundry at your place because she/he is trying to save money. You live alone and are responsible for all the bills. Do you allow them?

YES   NO

4. You are planning a party, and invited the guests already, but the stress of planning a party creates a lot of distress and mental strain. Do you still plan it because you want to please people by having this party to attend?

YES   NO

5. You have a medical appointment, and someone wants you to travel during this time. Do you choose to travel?

YES   NO

6. You have many responsibilities to complete today for example cooking for the family, cleaning, laundry, etc, but you are feeling like you will have a mental breakdown. Do you still complete the responsibilities?

YES   NO

7. You need your alone time for self-care and mental health, but your friends want to hang out. Do you choose to hang out with your friend?

YES   NO

8. Your friend has hurt you. You want to get revenge for the pain, but walking away and choosing peace over revenge is much harder. Do you choose to revenge?

YES   NO

9. Someone has hurt you over and over and over again, but you think they will change. Do you stay with them and continue to hope for change?

YES   NO

10. You do so much for the people you love, and they miss out on all your important events. Do you continue your relationship with them? Even if it's family?

YES   NO

These are the important questions that you need to ask yourself before you make any decisions. If you answered YES to any of these questions, you need to reevaluate your priorities, which should be you. The last one is a tricky one. Explore and connect to this one. Remember people come into your life for a reason, for a season, or for a lifetime.

-17-

Learn New Habits

17. Learn New Habits

Education is priceless. Education is power. You can educate yourself to create new habits which can equal the new you. Having a habit is a behavior done with little to no thought. The best way to form a new habit is to tie it to an existing one. Developing a habit is a simple form of learning and changing your behavior with experience.

Knowing what I knew growing up, I was a stranger to compelling myself into a successful life. I was stuck with old habits. I focused my attention more on social media rather than trying to elevate myself. I watched drama-filled reality TV shows such as *Love and Hip-Hop* and *Basketball Wives*. I mean, I was entertained, but this was not healthy. Thank God I decided to change my cable availability programs and this channel was no longer available. Overall, I wasted a lot of time that I could have been working on myself. Imagine all this time wasted when I could have been doing something productive. You are what you invest your time in.

I had an old habit of drinking excessively. I would tell myself that there was no point in drinking if I could not feel it. That if I was going to drink all these calories, I better feel the alcohol. I would label myself as a binge drinker. At almost every party or event, I would drink. Yes, I would definitely consider myself a social person, but I did not want to be socially drinking every time I would hang out with people.

I decided to do sober months. My first sober month was February 2022. This went so great and I felt so much better. Because of this I was attracting more things in my career and at the beginning of March I moved into my new place in Hingham. Talk about rewards for not drinking!

I went back to drinking, but soon I wanted to change things around again. I did another sober month in August 2022.

During August, I was able to take the kids to more places such as Cape Cod, dog-sat my brother's dog that my kids loved, and I had a fantastic time at Encore Casino in Somerville. I accomplished so many things, such as writing this book, getting the kids ready to start school, and going on my first trip with the kids to New York City! This was amazing! I had thought August was the wrong time to choose to be sober because I wanted to enjoy my summer nights with drinks, but it went so well that it continued into September. I am beyond grateful.

Another new habit that I learned was to create a morning routine. At 5 am, I would wake up and meditate. At 5:30 I would enjoy my coffee by myself before the kids woke up. I also started making my bed. I purchased new covers which created a better, cleaner look in my entire room. Tranquility.

Previously, I would slack on my gym time because I would rather spend time with my boyfriend, which would always upset me because I was ignoring my needs. Instead, now, I go for my morning workout right after I drop my kids off at the bus stop. This gives me more energy during the day, allows me to fulfill my needs, makes my day longer and more productive, and has helped me stay in shape and be healthy. This really works great for my mental health, too.

I started to appreciate more things around me. Sometimes I think about my past and all the things my ex did for me. At that time I did not appreciate it as much as I do today. I did not know how to appreciate it. Once, he went out to the store and bought me seven dresses just so when he brought them home I had one I could choose that I liked. I hated all of them! This was so mean of me. The first expensive purse he purchased for me was a Burberry. He went out of his way and treated me and I did not appreciate it. I only knew how to complain.

Now, I appreciate everything I have. The small things like the penny turned heads up for good luck. Appreciating that I can afford food to eat and have a place to live. Appreciating the rain when it pours and the sun when it shines. Appreciating someone offering me water. Oh, how I appreciate the little things now, and much more.

Most importantly I educated myself on healthy relationships. I learned communication skills so I could verbally express my feelings and communicate my needs and wants. If these were not met, I also learned to walk away.

With the excitement of a new relationship, I learned to take things slow. My ex-husband proposed to me in 10 days, and my first boyfriend got a tattoo of my name after just one month of being a couple. I've learned to slow down and go at my pace. I educated myself on dating, men, and what I wanted.

I decided I could no longer allow that to blind me. I know they say it takes three months to get to know a person because it's true, but it took me five months to walk away. So as of today, I am still working on this habit of dating, commitment, and control.

I learned to listen. I allowed people to talk instead of responding fast. There is so much information a person can provide you. Talking allowed me to understand the result of my actions. I did not believe anyone until I saw actions supporting their theories.

I learned to respond and not react. This new habit was the best I could have taken on. This helped me improve my self-control. It also allowed me to become emotionally intelligent which led to more professional and communicative relationships.

I educated myself on how to control my thoughts from thinking like the past. This new habit took a lot of patience and dedication. Every time I had a negative thought about myself or my life, I tried to find the positive. It is like a battle in your brain.

If I could not control my impulsive negative thoughts, I would speak positive affirmations into existence. If this did not work, I meditated or spoke to a friend and had that friend support me, not judge me, and bring me back to see the good. Like they say: Control your thoughts, control your life.

A new habit I had to learn was how to develop boundaries. What I will not tolerate anymore and how to walk away. I learned how to say no instead of agreeing with what people wanted from me.

I also taught myself about red flags, manipulation, love bombing, gaslighting, and breadcrumbing. The first sign of these, oh, your time is up and I am moving on. I began allowing the flow of new healthy relationship patterns.

I educated myself about feminine power and how to receive. Instead of being in my masculine energy all the time and knowing I can provide for myself and my family, I allowed others to help me. Instead of doing things myself all the time, I asked for help. If a man wants to offer me help, I take it. Ladies, please, you do not have to give anything in return. If a man wants to help allow him. Allow yourself to receive and appreciate the small things they do without feeling compelled to do anything in return.

Maintaining a new habit requires research and building the new habit into your schedule. Using this as guidance, give yourself rewards for the goals you reach. New habits equal a new you.

Educate yourself on what kind of person you want to be and what new habits you want to have (in replace of old ones). My sister-in-law, Anna, told me a great story about a woman who had to quit smoking. This woman associated her drinking coffee with having a cigarette. She replaced her habit of drinking coffee with drinking tea, and then no longer associated it with smoking a cigarette. She was then able to quit smoking. This way she programmed a new routine into her schedule and life and received different outcomes.

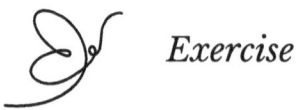 *Exercise*

Start a healthy habit in 10 days.

Old Habit _____

Replace with

New Habit _____

Try to do this every one to three months. Substituting one old habit with one new habit.

-18-

Require Healthy Relationships

Step 18 - Require Healthy Relationships

What are healthy relationships? In a healthy relationship, you respect each other's independence and can make decisions without fear. Open communication is the root of all healthy relationships. This takes effort from both parties. Once you attain that then you can attract healthy relationships and require a certain treatment for yourself. People who have healthy relationships feel happier and are more satisfied with their lives. They are less likely to have physical and mental problems. Healthy relationships can increase your sense of worth and belonging and help you feel less alone.

The first step to having healthy relationships is to have a healthy relationship with yourself. Growing up I did not have a healthy relationship with myself. I mean how was I supposed to be in a healthy relationship with myself when no one taught me, when I never saw one, nor was I brought up around one? I witnessed and grew up around domestic violence that I thought was normal. It was normal to be unhealthy and toxic.

From what I can remember I was brought up around a lot of abuse and because of this I experienced the abuse myself. Physical abuse, mental abuse, verbal abuse, financial abuse, emotional abuse, and sexual abuse. I have developed PTSD from all the unhealthy relationships I witnessed and was involved in. To me, this was all I knew and was familiar with.

I started developing a healthy relationship with myself. I learned that starting a healthy relationship with yourself is finding out the things you like, enjoy doing, and how to treat yourself. I found joy in the little things such as a hot coffee in the morning, or a walk along the beach. I meditated every morning. I started to focus on my inner world. I started to value myself.

I made this a new habit. Today, for instance, I took myself on a romantic picnic to watch the sunset on Nantasket Beach. I wrote in my journal about the amazing time I was having in my life by taking myself out, meeting new people, and attending a charity event. I was becoming my best friend.

I developed a healthy relationship with myself where I knew how I wanted to be treated by others. I started to make myself a priority and take care of my needs.

After developing a healthy relationship with myself, I researched how to be in a healthy relationship with others. I now have four requirements: Respect, safety, trust, and full communication.

I am able to make decisions regarding my independence and my own happiness without feeling bad. I have developed a safe environment for myself where it requires everyone to keep their hands to themselves. Only kind words are used. Trust is a huge factor in any type of relationship. Only the truth may be spoken, even if it's tense. I require being softly spoken to, and mental support is a must.

I have also reprogrammed my subconscious to have and develop healthy relationships. I no longer tolerate disrespect, lying, or any form of negativity surrounding me. If I feel like I sense any wrongdoing in my life by someone, or see red flags, I have no problem walking away and blocking them. Want to see my block list? A healthy life is all I want to live because when you have health you have everything.

I would suggest healing your old relationship with yourself and others and developing a new one with the tools and exercises in this book.

Your first healthy relationship has to be focused on yourself. The rest will come. There is no rush in the healing of the old relationship you experienced that may still have an effect today.

You have to forgive yourself, realize your faults as well as your strengths, and where you went wrong. Remember if a relationship does not feel right or is giving you anxiety, take time away from it and continue being the best version of yourself.

 *Activity*

Watch and reflect on the video below.

-19-

Take Pressure Off

Step 19 - Take Pressure Off

There is so much pressure for us to succeed. So much pressure to complete and meet deadlines. To make things happen. To get things done. To do well. This pressure can cause us to feel mentally and physically stressed and drained. It can lead us to feel overwhelmed.

As I wrote this book, I felt pressure. I felt pressured to write every day. To make it my best. I felt pressure to complete it before my next meeting with my publisher. I felt pressure to write while I was on vacation because I could not enjoy my vacation as much as I wanted to because I felt like I needed to write. The pressure to write took the present moment away. I am supposed to be what I preach! So, why was I putting all this pressure on myself?

Most of the time I put pressure on myself when I am in my head, thinking way into the future. As I am writing this, I am on vacation and I am still putting pressure on myself to write! It is hard to let myself loose to enjoy the beauty of Provincetown, Cape Cod because of the pressure I put on myself to write.

I'm choosing to let myself write. So here I am, typing on vacation! I need to do this for myself because when I feel like I have accomplished something it takes some pressure off of my current state. It helps me feel balanced. So I write. I meditate. And I take some breaths, being okay with where I am.

Sometimes writing can take some pressure off and help me feel at ease. It's a coping mechanism. It helps to get everything out on paper. And it feels good to achieve a goal.

God puts us in every situation for a reason. We are all human. We get in our thoughts sometimes, and for me, it is because of my past trauma and the pressure to succeed.

I now recollect the times when I put so much pressure on myself. To think of places to take my kids to entertain them. To go out with my friends or hang out with my boyfriend. To go to the gym every day. You know what advice I'd give myself now? It's ok to just do nothing.

If you have kids, let them watch tv for a little bit so you can have your rest. When your friends want you to go out, it's ok to say no and have a night to yourself. If you feel pressure to go to the gym, it's ok to skip a day or two. If your boyfriend/girlfriend wants to hang out with you all the time it's ok to ask for some space. When working on a project, allow yourself to also enjoy life.

Allow your body to rest. Allow your mind to rejuvenate. Having priorities for yourself helps a lot when taking the pressure off. Prioritize yourself and your needs. When you commit to something you want to do, it takes a lot of pressure off. Sometimes we put too much pressure on our current situation, but letting go and trusting the journey releases the pressure, the anxiety, and feeling back to normal. Putting pressure on an outcome only affects your well-being and we need to take care of that first.

Ways to Deal with Pressure:

1. Stay focused and complete what needs to be accomplished.

2. Breathe.

3. Slow down.

4. Utilize your vacation time wisely.

5. Write down what's bothering you.

6. Remain calm.

7. Stay positive.

8. Set boundaries.

9. Take time off for yourself.

10. Learn to say no.

11. Seek support from a friend or family member.

 *Exercise*

Watch and reflect on the video below.

-20-

Listen to the Angels

Step 20 - Listen to the Angels

Ever heard of angel numbers? Or make a wish at 11:11? These repetitive sequences of numbers are significant. The numbers carry with them a certain energy or meaning in the universe. You usually see them when you are experiencing a random thought. Angel numbers are just one way of thinking about the world and gaining clarity. This is the divine trying to tell you something. You are being sent guidance on what is happening in your life.

I began looking for the meaning behind the numbers I was seeing. My marital house number was 236. Look at the meaning of this number: 236 is only associated with people who influence your life in the right way. This number also says to focus on improving every aspect of your life. How ironic! This number was my old, marital, house number. Where, due to the restraining order that I filed, the wrong people were removed and no longer visited. No more old friends coming over with bad intentions. No more fights or arguing with the previous people that had access to the home. Definitely, no more gatherings of people who said I should stay in this unhealthy relationship because they did not support divorce or my dreams. This number spoke volumes.

After the people who were wrong for me were removed, this allowed the people who were right for me to enter. More relationships with people who were a positive influence on me were guided into my life. I developed good and supportive friendships that I allowed into my home. These were people who cared about each other and helped each other grow. This felt amazing and very uplifting.

I started to refocus on every aspect of my life. I stood up for myself and for my rights. I had courage. I had freedom, and most importantly I had health. I believe this was spiritually guided.

I focused on improving my life by consistently working on my mental health by continuing meditation, therapy, and healthy eating. I worked on my body at the gym. Being healthy physically had so many benefits and allowed me to feel good. This allowed me to be guided by improving my surroundings with positive and happy people that supported me and my dreams. I focused on my ambitions, such as working with my friend on my website and improving my new image as the real Angelika Kilian. I wanted to be someone, someone important, someone I knew I always was.

Now I live at number 203. This number represents completion. I am fully complete in my life and this is where I belong. Living in my dream town. I ended a cycle. I always say that 203 is where my new life, the real life that I always wanted to live, started. This has opened up self-expression, creativity, talents, optimism, and joy in my life.

Self-expression: I am fully able to express how I feel, what I think, what bothers me, what I like, and have a full-on conversation. It feels amazing to express myself and be heard. People listen to me and feel inspired. I can finally do the things I love and share with the world and make a positive influence. The best thing is that I am fully expressive and no longer care what the negative people or the people that tried to control me think of me. I am being myself and this is who I am.

Creativity: I have become very creative at my new place. I created the lifestyle I always wanted. Living in a luxury apartment, living in a rich neighborhood, and creating the dream of my life. I created videos and became invited by Meta to become a digital creator on Facebook. I used my newfound creativity to find solutions and change my life.

Talents: The more talents I have the more successful I have become. I have created and developed a new talent for writing, as well as a new talent for making videos. I always say God gave you a talent, now multiply it, and you will have more so you can achieve more. I developed new skills that help me grow and achieve the things I want. (Matthew 25:14–30)

Communication, optimism, and joy: I can tell you I am very happy where I am in life. I love to communicate effectively and it benefited me in achieving many business ventures. I love now that I can communicate my feelings, my needs, and wants, and definitely honor my space when I need it.

This example is based on the number of the place I live at now: 203. As I mentioned earlier, angel numbers are guidance.

When you see a sequence number, automatically go back to what you were thinking and find the spiritual meaning of it and your answer should be right there. These angel numbers can pop up anywhere. On your clock, on your receipt, on a car license plate, and even on a building or house number you may be driving by.

I want you to pay very close attention to when you see a sequence of numbers. Connect what you were thinking about at the time to the numbers you saw and research the meaning. This can signify anything to you such as your love life, your current position, and confirm things you have questions about. It's guidance and confirmation in angel numbers.

You can start learning about angel numbers and the meaning behind them. Keep making your wishes at 11:11. It's actually really fun.

 *Exercise*

Google the spiritual meaning of the number of the place where you live. Look at what it states. Any connections? Write the spiritual meaning behind it below or in your journal.

Research all of these numbers to learn their spiritual angel meanings.

111 _____

222 _____

333 _____

444 _____

555 _____

666 _____

777 _____

888 _____

999 _____

-21-

Journal

Step 21. Journal

Journaling is the most therapeutic way to help you create order when your world feels like it's in chaos. Journaling allows you to write down your emotions and feelings and release them. Journaling is a great way to record your daily thoughts and experiences. This allows you to also write things you are going through when you cannot talk to anyone. In fact, journaling can help you achieve goals, track your progress and growth, gain self-confidence, improve writing and communication skills, reduce stress and anxiety, find inspiration, strengthen memory, and create a stream of consciousness.

Allow me to randomly choose a page from my journal and share it with you.

10/18/21

Full moon, every day is a Best Day.

Meditated on focus and creativity today. It started as a joyous day.

Dropped off Max at school on time.

Did Covid-19 testing before fitting for a movie.

Spent quality time with Damian and watched Polish cartoons. Grateful for the opportunity that I can make some extra money doing DoorDash while the kids are in school.

Received a child tax check and a letter that I can apply for my loan.

Took myself and the kids shopping. Received $4 off at Old Navy. I forgive myself for being angry with them in the store. Sometimes it's way too much! I know this was a test of how I realize and respond to my emotions. Well, all I can say is that I improved.

God is so good to me. I was so blessed today. I felt every blessing with my heart. My heart was so full I could have started crying.

I have tears in my eyes because every time I think about my past I look at how far I came. God, you have been so good to me. Thank you.

Yoanna called me today. She is such a good soul. She called to tell me I am on her mind and that she sends positive and blessing energy toward me. I definitely felt that! She wanted to help me to find ways I can make extra money. She is so sweet.

I am so blessed and grateful for my new life, my genuine and true friends, and all the amazing things that I have had to go through. I am so blessed and grateful for my healthy children. I am trying to be the best mother I can.

Journaling has allowed me to discover myself even more. The more I wrote, the more I appreciated my life—the good, the bad, and the things I could not control. I journaled everything. I journaled my days. I journaled when I was feeling angry or smitten with love. I journaled my wants. I journaled all the things I wanted to become (in the present tense, of course). I journaled everything I was grateful for. I journaled when I cried. This was so therapeutic for me when I did not want to share certain parts of my life with others, but I could not keep them inside because it felt like bad energy. Writing made things better and made me feel better.

Journaling is such a beautiful thing. Create a writing routine in your life. I would recommend writing before you go to sleep. This way, you can reflect on your day. Include discoveries, things that stood out, things you learned about yourself, and things that happened to you that you are grateful for. Write anything you want to talk about, share, learn, or complete.

 *Exercise*

Write down what you can take away from today in your journal.

-22-

Spirit Leads the Way

Step 22 - Spirit Leads the Way

Spirit is a guidance system that comes from within you. Spirit helps lead you through signs, songs, visual sightings, and many other ways of communicating with you.

Living day-to-day, I receive messages through things I hear or see. Recently my boys have been singing "Toxic" by BoyWithUke. I told them to stop since it was a negative song. They kept singing it and I realized there was a meaning behind this. At that moment in time, my friends were toxic, just like the song says! I was too wrapped up in being there for my friends that I was under so much pressure that I started to lose myself. Now this made sense, my friends were toxic to my health so I had to get some space. I had to focus on myself and my needs.

Another time spirit gave me a message to rest. I had a grocery bag fall on my toe. Dang did that hurt. As I am a person that loves to wear heels and always look my best, I could not go out anywhere until I recovered from my hurt toe. I was in so much pain that I had to go to the emergency room to relieve the pressure. Spirit wanted me to rest and take care of myself.

Sometimes I will catch pieces of conversations and the words that I hear are like a light to my life. One time I was at the pool lounging and I heard two ladies talking about a wedding in February. Then it clicked. If I ever wanted to get married it would be in February because I want to get married when it snows out and February is the perfect month.

Another way that Spirit communicates with me is through numbers. The number 24 is a significant number to me, because this is the night before the day we celebrate the birth of Jesus, so to me the number is connected with new beginnings. The next day is the 25th, which is Christmas Day. I love Christmas. This is my favorite holiday.

This day, the 25th, has significance. I was married on May 25, 2013. After my divorce, the first relationship I was in that became official was on May 25, 2022.

May is the fifth month. The number five means balance. This also connects to my brother's house, where I recovered from my surgery, which is 55, and my physical therapy address which is 55 also. Spirit is telling me that during these times I was balanced. Do you see where I am going with this? Spirit tries to communicate with you.

The biggest sign I received was this one right here in the photo below. I was walking the beach on my birthday, April 7, and out of all the days I walked on the same beach, I saw these drawings. Spirit was communicating. I came across this on my birthday in 2021. The signs told me that I will be a star, I will be rich, and I will find true unconditional love. Well, as I write this, I am a star, I am rich and I found true unconditional love; all within myself. It's like these signs that spirit could manifest this for me. I was always told I am a fast manifester. I always believed.

For example, when I have plans to go somewhere, like a party, or event, and my anxiety is through the roof, this is when Spirit is trying to communicate to me that I do not need to go. Once I decide not to go, I feel the pressure and stress automatically lift. If it's meant to be, even in a relationship, you should feel at ease and feel like yourself. If you are feeling out of alignment, pressured, anxious, or forced to go somewhere or be with someone and your body is rejecting it, this is Spirit trying to communicate to you to just stay put and signal you not to take part in this situation.

Spirit is so powerful at communicating with you that it gives you signs. These are signs of things you need to confirm, signs to guide you, or signs to confirm your future. Communication can come through people, songs, or colors. You just have to allow yourself to see what the spirit is trying to tell you. This will get easier over time. The easiest way to tell when Spirit is trying to communicate to you is when you are under pressure and discombobulated and stressed out about what you are "forced to do." That's when Spirit is telling you not to force the outcome. When it's time it will happen and you should feel at peace, and allow it to happen naturally. Alignment.

 *Exercise*

I have an exercise for you to see how Spirit speaks to you and how to spot signs. Think about something that you have been wanting, praying for, or dreaming about. Now check what today's day is. Write down what this day's spiritual meaning is. After that connect it to what you have been wanting, praying, or dreaming about.

What interpretation can you make? Write about this in your journal or in the space below.

Now think of a color. Write its spiritual meaning. Now write how this can be connected to your life.

Next, turn on a song—the first one that pops into your head. Think about how your life can connect to this song. Write all the positive things you see for yourself from this song.

-23-

Patience is a Virtue

Step 23 - Patience is a Virtue

Patience is the ability to wait without becoming annoyed, upset, or angry. It's when you exercise self-control rather than lashing out and complaining. Practicing patience is all about how you act. Being patient is easiest when we make a choice to slow down. We must make a conscious choice to slow down the processes that are going on in our minds, wills, and emotions. Patience is allowing things to happen.

I wish I had had more patience about waiting to get married. I always wanted to get married young (21 years old). Should I have waited? Maybe. But I got what I wanted. I was married to the man that I have two beautiful boys with. Do I regret it? Absolutely not. Everything happens for a reason and at God's perfect timing. If I did not get married I would have not learned the lessons I have. I wouldn't have my beautiful, healthy children and be a young mom.

Now, I can say that being patient and waiting for the right partner is so worth it. You discover so much about yourself— your standards, your self-worth, your wants, and many more things.

During my separation from my ex-husband, I focused on myself. I did not date. I was scared of men and I was scared of dating. My friends insisted that I go on a date for a free dinner or just for the experience of it, but the thought of entertaining that person did not sit well with me. I preferred to be alone and I just enjoyed hearing about my girlfriends' experiences of their dating life.

My girlfriends would share their dating stories, of the amazing places they went, the amazing restaurants they dined at, and the flowers and gifts they received. I was happy for them and felt a little jealous, but it was my choice to not date. I had not found anyone to give my time to. I was still not ready.

I finally did the dating app thing and deleted it after two days. That was totally not for me. Then I took myself on dates hoping I would run into a wonderful man in person while I was out. I did meet a couple of people. I gave them my number to break out of my shell and go on dates. Obviously, I was not ready to pursue anything further, because I ended up blocking their number.

Was it worth waiting this whole time to date? Yes. Was it worth being alone to discover and heal yourself? Yes. Was it worth all the tears? Yes. Definitely worth being patient for.

While waiting, God was only preparing me for the good things that were meant to happen in my life. God had to allow me to be by myself so He could strengthen me and make me wiser. He gave me tests and tools and allowed me to build into the woman I always wanted to become. He allowed me to see my worth and strength, my good, and my purpose, and allowed me to see and accept the real me.

Having patience is an amazing quality. This allowed me to become a better person, a better mother to my children, a better friend, and a better me. This allowed things to happen in my life the way they were supposed to and my reaction to them allowed me to be receiving and accepting without putting up a fight. Patience allowed me to be more calm and more positive.

Patience teaches you a lesson. It taught me the powerful lesson that I did not need anyone to complete me. Patience allows things to happen at the right time for the right reasons. So be patient, especially with your body, mind, and soul. This is your most valuable asset. Be patient and allow this time to self-reflect and discover yourself. Patience is a virtue.

During your alone time, be patient with yourself and allow good things to enter. Work on yourself or focus on anything you want to achieve. This will come at the right time and you will thank yourself for waiting. Remember, patience is not a punishment, it's a learning lesson, a seasoning period of learning and improving yourself so you can attract the life of your dreams and be ready for it when it comes.

A year had passed since I had been separated. I cried to God that I was ready for someone. That I am ready to receive and be in love. That I was ready to date. I told God that the first person that would ask me out, I would go out with.

Six days passed and I had a man named Jon come to help install my refrigerator. We talked and began to see each other daily. It was so nice to know someone because I was new to the neighborhood. After the third time hanging out, Jon brought a highway sign in front of my balcony that he had personally written, "Will you go out on a date with me Angelika?" I said, "Yes!"

It was on May 25, 2022, that I went out on my first date after my separation. As I shared before in chapter 20, this day has so much significance for me that it's unreal. Jon picked me up in his big, white truck. I waited outside until he opened the door for me. While driving he pulled out a little box. He knew I loved gifts. This is my love language. I opened it and it was a white gold cross with a half-carat diamond! I was so happy I cried because this was exactly what I asked for on my birthday and no one bought it for me. How did he know me so well already? I loved it!

We arrived at the Norwood Memorial Airport. As a first date, Jon took me on a helicopter ride over the ocean on the South Shore. This was beyond breathtaking: the ocean, sunset, and an amazing time.

As we landed, we were waiting for what I thought would be a golf cart to drive us back to his truck. I saw a white limo drive our way. I couldn't believe it! He booked a limo for our first date! Oh, and that's not all, the limo had a red carpet and Jon also hired professional photographers to capture the whole moment. It was beyond my wildest dreams.

The limo drove us to dinner at Morton's Steakhouse at the Seaport in Boston. This was the perfect ending to our date. The company was amazing and the food was great. We celebrated by drinking champagne and the conversations just flowed. Jon and I were having such an amazing time that we were the last ones to leave the restaurant. What a magnificent and magical first date.

 Challenge

Here is a challenge for you to learn patience and the benefits of waiting. This patience will require you to work on yourself to become a better individual in order to attract the things you want and need in your life. When you are patient good things happen naturally because you attract these to you. When you are forcing the outcome the backlash is 10x greater and will take longer to receive the things and life you desire.

I want you to challenge yourself and choose one challenge out of these three. You could also choose to do all three or add your own challenge.

Challenge #1: Do not date for three months after your last relationship. If you were married, give yourself one year. This is why: When you are in a relationship you become comfortable with the life and lifestyle you share with that person. Your activities together become a habit or a routine. Date nights, social gatherings, and spending time with each other. Now the breakup might hurt, but giving yourself time allows you to refocus on yourself, reflect on where you need to improve yourself and fill in the void of being by yourself and not your partner. You are finding yourself and developing self-growth.

Challenge #2: Exercise for two months straight. I do not mean you have to go hard at the gym every day, but I do expect you to be consistent for two months. Walk, do yoga, take classes, something that will get you moving almost every single day. This will be time invested in you, your mind, and your body. The amount of time and energy you invest in your exercise is the result you will have in your self-improvement.

Challenge #3: Every day for one month, write something positive about yourself or something positive you did.

You got this!

-24-

Being Grateful

Step 24 - Being Grateful

Being grateful is a positive emotion. It involves being thankful and appreciative of what you have or have been through. It leads you to a positive change in yourself. Gratitude is associated with several mental and physical health benefits. When you experience gratitude, you are feeling thankful for something or someone in your life.

As a single mother, I was having a difficult time paying for oil. It was the winter of 2021. I called the oil assistance at the Quincy Community Action Program (QCAP) Resource Center in Quincy where I was referred to by DCF. I submitted my application. It was Friday and my oil was gone. I did not know how long the application process would take. I could not stay home because it was too cold. I did not have hot water. I did not do laundry or turn on the dishwasher so I could save the last bits of oil for my children. I slept over at my friend's house over the weekend and took showers at the gym while my kids were with their dad.

As I came home on Monday. I checked my mail. I saw a pink slip. It was an oil slip. My tank has been filled! I cried. I cried because this was a little miracle God had given me. I was beyond grateful. I was beyond happy. I couldn't believe I had received oil in that small amount of time. A full tank of oil. I could provide a warm home for my children just in time as I was getting them back later on that day. Little things like this bring so much relief and joy to your life. I will never forget this. This felt like Christmas.

Even though I was struggling, I appreciated the struggle. I appreciated every moment of my life because in my eyes I had everything. I had good health, a home to live in, food to eat, family, and good friends.

I felt very grateful for my family and my close friends during this time. I was grateful to my family for understanding and supporting me through this situation and not choosing sides. Some family members even lent me money to get back on my feet.

I also had a full appreciation for my friends during this time, who supported me emotionally, were there for me mentally, and always lifted my spirits.

Even though my PTSD creeps up on me, I appreciate this as a gift, too. This allows me to advocate for mental health and show support to others.

Every morning I thank God I am alive. I am grateful I have overcome so much fear of leaving a toxic relationship, of living by myself, and finding ways to support myself and my children. I am grateful for the life lessons that I was taught during this time, the self-discoveries, and the changes. These situations were the best things that could have happened in my life. If it wasn't for this downfall I would not be where I am today—a better person, happier, free, and living my dream life.

Showing appreciation for what you have allows you to feel better and notice the small things that make a huge change and impact on your life. When you can show gratitude for the things that you already have, then you will be ready to receive more. Show appreciation for all the people in your life. They made a difference in your life and you make a difference in theirs. Showing gratitude for what you already have already takes you to another place—a higher place in your heart, in your head, your life. Be grateful and show gratitude.

 *Exercise*

List ten things you are grateful for:

1.

2.

3.

4.

5.

6.

7.

8.

9.

10.

Now I want you to text or call someone and show your gratitude for them. Watch what happens and how you feel.

-25-

Welcome Abundance

Step 25 - Welcome Abundance

Abundance is having a large quantity of something. You can have abundance in your career, abundance in money, abundance in love, abundance in health, and abundance in life. It can look like a change in your life for the better. A fullness in joy, spirit, and soul.

Think of it like this. You plant a seed. If you are a good person and feed yourself with positivity and health, your seed will grow. If you feed yourself with positivity, goals, and things that make you happy, you will prosper and receive abundance in those areas of life. As they say, what you sow is what you grow. When you grow it comes back to you abundantly.

During my divorce, I was living in our mansion, as a single mother, with my two sons, but I could barely afford anything. My ex-husband had been the breadwinner in our household, and I now had no access to our bank accounts. I was in $74K in debt from my marriage, and living on credit cards. I had the debt because when we purchased the home, I took on our marital debt so my ex, who purchased the house, had a better debt-to-income ratio on paper.

As time went on, I was finally approved for government assistance where I was given food stamps. With that help, I could purchase plenty of food to feed my children without the worry of not having enough. Thank God for government assistance. I was blessed abundantly, and I no longer had to lean on strangers to help me out with food.

I was grateful that I had a place to live. And when my ex decided to sell the house, God blessed me abundantly with a new place. I was able to move with my two boys to a place that has a pool and a gym and is within walking distance of restaurants, shops, the ocean, and new friends.

The marital debt I took on was cut down to $53K thanks to a debt consolidation company. I was able to get even better settlements with my debt and pay it off with a small amount every two weeks.

My investments also started to pay off. I never thought I would imagine making over six figures in one year! From having no money and no job, I was blessed abundantly with movie roles, extra money doing liquor promos, and connections with people that allowed me to find ways for me to prosper.

When I divorced, I was granted primary custody, awarded child support, and given half of the house profits.

I have always told myself that any bad situation or struggle is temporary, but needed. I like to think that I always had everything because I was alive and healthy and this was enough to make a difference in my life.

Living life abundantly, I became happy and confident in everything I did. I became abundant in the best way possible, being the real me and appreciating what I have and where I am in life. Once I healed, I was ready to receive. I stopped expecting anything and began allowing abundance to flow in.

I believe abundance happens when you contribute your time and effort to things that are life-changing in positive ways. In things that make you feel good and happy. In areas that make you a better person and the best version of yourself. True to yourself and the person you know you really are.

Abundance only happens if you put in the work. Focus on working on yourself and contributing to the world around you. You cannot force an outcome. You have to be patient and never give up.

Have you ever seen a flower grow or the process a butterfly has to go through? It's a journey and takes time to get the results you want, but be patient because abundance will come to full bloom.

 *Activity*

Here are 10 affirmations that will help you affirm the abundance that you are going to receive. Please re-write them on a piece of paper and place the paper where you can see it every day.

I am worthy of what I desire.

I have everything I need to be successful.

I am open to limitless possibilities.

I achieve whatever I set my mind to.

I believe in myself.

I am ready to share my gifts with the world.

I surrender to receive what is already mine.

I attract miracles into my life.

I am open to receiving unexpected opportunities.

I am grateful for the abundance that I already have.

-26-

Refocus and Shift

Step 26 - Refocus and Shift

With life, many distractions come as you try to succeed and build an empire. It is important to stay focused and make shifts on the things you are needing to accomplish your goals. This focus should be consistent. Focusing and staying attentive and true to your goals will allow you to shift back to reaching your dream. Remember why you started! Think positively. Keep going. Do not give up.

I was distracted while writing this book. I had a new boyfriend. You know how that goes—infatuation, wanting to spend time with him, going on dates, fulfilling each other's needs, traveling. Especially at the beginning stages, these things can take priority. I put my focus on him instead of finishing my book. I realized I needed to shift my current situation and take my energy back and take a break from everything and refocus on myself.

I also had friends that wanted to come over, and I spent time hosting them at my place. My children needed my attention and I needed to conduct my responsibilities as a mother. I had a lot on my plate—friends, kids, work, and writing my book. It was a lot to balance with no time to myself.

I look at my oldest son. Sometimes when he is doing homework, he gets distracted. I tell him to refocus and shift back to what he was working on. To focus on the present moment and engage. It's a way of retraining the brain to get things accomplished instead of putting them off. When a small task such as a homework assignment is completed you feel great about yourself. You completed what you needed to and now you can rest. Enjoy. Rejuvenate. Watch tv. You earned it.

I've learned to put my priorities first, accomplishing what I have to first, before going out, having a drink, and traveling.

As long as I get things done and stay focused on my dreams and goals I can then reward myself. When I get distracted I have to shift my reality and remind myself why I started.

I make sure that I always come back to what I invested in. I invested in helping others and seeing people succeed. I couldn't slack on this. I want this for you, too. If I am successful, you are too. Remember how I said you have to pour into your cup first so it overflows? I have to be the best version of myself and live my dream so I can give you my tools and have you succeed in life and fulfill your wildest dreams, too.

Everything has a time and place. What I have learned is that I had to refocus on my goals and shift my reality. For instance, if it wasn't for my emotional breakdown at the Cape that I wrote about in chapter 19, I would not have been as passionate about writing as I am now. When I refocused and shifted my energy to accomplishing what I wanted, even when I was on vacation, I felt satisfaction within myself. Sometimes, we have to take a break from what we are doing and complete what we have to do. This way we can feel the satisfaction of completing a goal without sabotaging the present moment. We are only human.

Refocusing and shifting back to remembering my accomplishments was essential. This allowed time for me to focus and finish the things I started. I now had alone time and was able to enjoy things that I want to do to get where I am going. If I made it this far I want to keep going and risk it all, rather than getting this far and giving up. Refocusing and reshifting my energy back to my goals also allowed me to become more disciplined in myself and my life. This also made me prioritize things too. I might get sidetracked with everything that is going on in my life, but I always remind myself what really needs to be done.

If you tend to prioritize other people's needs and desires over your own, I suggest limiting your time going out or hanging out with people until you get your work done. You are your own success story. It is up to you to stay focused on your goals and shift to what is bringing them closer to you.

Exercise

Write down things you are currently working on. Like a "to-do" list:

1.

2.

3.

4.

5.

Write down the actions you are taking toward these goals.

1.

2.

3.

4.

5.

How will you reward yourself when you accomplish these goals?

1.

2.

3.

4.

5.

Write down what else you need to do to accomplish these goals.

1.

2.

3.

4.

5.

What is preventing you from reaching these goals?

1.

2.

3.

4.

5.

How can you focus and shift back toward these goals?

1.

2.

3.

4.

5.

Refocus and Shift. Make it happen.

-27-

Dream and Grow

Step 27 - Dream and Grow

When you dream you are creating thoughts, images, and sensations in your mind and body. Growth refers to the self-improvement of your skills, knowledge, personal qualities, life, and outlook to help you fully reach your dream life. When you grow you are attracting these things to take place in your conscious reality. Dream and grow.

For most of 2021, I was financially struggling. As I went shopping for food, I made sure to stick to my budget of $50. As I stood in line at Stop & Shop I scanned the card and it was declined. I stood there ready to walk away empty-handed. A woman behind me offered to pay for my groceries. I told her my story and she responded that she has been there before. I cried as she paid for me. I felt like I was in a movie.

Having my ex ask to take the children on vacation after vacation made me feel horrible. My ex had more time with our children because I could not afford to take them places so I allowed them to travel with their dad. I did not want to take away their fun and be with me where I could not provide much at the time. I did not want my children to see me struggle.

Every month or so I would have to watch and accept my ex taking them to Virginia, flying them to Chicago, going to New Jersey, and pursuing most of the children's requests, including material things. Taking them to Dave & Buster's, and so forth, while I did not have much of anything to take care of my children. I did not like not having money and I started to do something to improve my situation.

Being poor and broke was not part of my dream for my life. I knew who I was and decided to make the best of my situation and dreamed big. I lived like I was at my end result. I started to live like I already had it all.

I went to expensive stores such as Cartier and Chanel like I could afford those items and experienced the things I wanted and the life I wanted to live while creating a money mindset. I test-drove my dream car, a Range Rover Sport, like I already owned one.

This allowed me to form a new mindset and a path to success. It helped me to seek ways of getting here. I dressed and spoke very highly of myself and created high standards and a high monetary value for my modeling services like a celebrity model. I would act like I was already famous. I pretended that candid photos of me were by the paparazzi. With every small step toward my dream, I started to create and attract my new reality.

When I entered a restaurant or any place there was a line. I told myself that I was VIP and never waited in line and always asked for the best seats. I wanted the best. I spoke things into existence. I would say that I wanted to expand my talents and become a movie star. Now, here I am on my movie sets, acting like I am the star of the movie and cutting the lines for hair and makeup because I knew I was the star and that I deserved special treatment.

In 2021 I wrote all my biggest dreams on a piece of paper. The other day I looked at them. I started with 133 and I have checked off 64 of them, just within a year's mark. Some things that I accomplished I did not write down because they happened naturally which was destined for me toward my goals and the direction for my dreams.

The more I asked God for the life I wanted, the more he placed things, people, and events in my path to get me closer. I improved a lot in my mindset to create wealth and success by listening to Bob Proctor's seminars and videos. By meditating, I improved my confidence, self-worth, and possible achievements. By journaling, I improved my communication skills which led me to more networking opportunities. From meeting the right people, I was able to get ideas for my future success such as creating a plan to start making it big, hitting points like creating a website, growing my Instagram account, and writing this book.

By recording Youtube videos, I was able to expand my new skills and knowledge and improve my personal qualities, as well as share with others about reaching their dreams.

At the end of 2022, I went over my bank account statement. From having no money, overdraft fees on my bank accounts, borrowing money from people, and living on credit cards, I can share with you that with the change of my mindset and dreaming big like I was already at my end result, in 2022 I am proud to say I made six figures.

 *Challenge*

The best way I achieve my dreams is to act like I already have them. I dreamed big. Why dream small? I was given a dream because God knew that I could reach it and He made everything possible. There is a reason you have a dream.

I want you to start living your dream life like you already have it. Do not allow anything to hold you back from living it. Accept your situation, but never be it. Conquer your fear and step out of your comfort zone and start doing something for your life you have never done before. Do not be afraid of failure. Taking the first step of writing your dreams down on a piece of paper creates momentum for you to achieve.

What does your end result look like? Be very detailed. Write in your journal.

President's Wife

-28-

Trust Your Intuition

28. Trust Your Intuition

Intuition is a feeling. It allows you to understand something immediately without conscious reasoning. It is the power of something happening directly without any thought put in. The ability that makes it possible to know something without any proof or evidence. Trusting your intuition allows you to make better choices for yourself. It's listening to your own needs and trusting yourself.

I remember when I went with a male friend to a restaurant. I had known him for a while and wanted to meet with him to get a man's perspective on some things I was going through. I was highly disappointed with the restaurant he chose. Automatically, my intuition was telling me something wasn't right. Then I continued to tell myself, *it will be all right, he's my friend.*

As I went to see him that evening, I got this uncomfortable feeling and couldn't stop thinking, *why am I here?* I did not want to be there anymore. We continued to talk, and by the end of the night, our conversation finally started to flow. I thought *things are always awkward in the beginning.* The night ended and he asked for a ride home from me and invited me to see his place. I never drive a man home, especially late at night, so this did not feel right. But I thought, *oh, he's my friend.*

We got inside my car. We started to drive away, but I stopped immediately and told him I could not drive him home, that it did not feel right. I was having anxiety. He ended up ordering an Uber home and I went home with a very awkward feeling. I did not feel comfortable at all. I am so happy I followed my intuition and left the restaurant alone.

When following my intuition I go for what feels right. I trust my tension and anxiety as signs that something is not right. I like to feel at peace when making decisions and not have to feel forced to do something or go somewhere.

Right now, I am at a place where I trust my intuition when it tells me to focus on myself and distance myself from friends, social media, and other environments. Once I have created alone time with myself, my intuition escalated. I was no longer influenced by outside voices, opinions, or judgments.

When I feel discouraged or uneasy, that is my intuition telling me something's not right. Listening to myself first and making the right decisions for myself helps me with my mental health as well as eases my stress. If I am doing things for other people and my intuition is rowdy, well that's my sign right there to separate myself.

As you develop your intuition, I would highly recommend being by yourself when making decisions and exploring your feelings during this time. This is the only way to get stronger and better at this. Sometimes you make a choice, and when the choice is for you, go forward with it, even if it feels a little bit selfish. Your intuition should make you feel at peace, not experience force or any anxiety.

In the end, you will be happy you followed your intuition and made the right decision for yourself. Your intuition is there for a reason, and it's only to better the individual you are. Practice without reaching out to anyone for advice. Practice makes perfect.

Exercise

Write down current decisions you have to make.

The way to make an intuitive decision is to ask yourself these questions:

- Which one would make me happier?
- Which one do I feel moves toward peace?
- Which end result will I prefer?

Tune into your responses to each question, and then write down your choice.

Now ask yourself, how do you feel in response? Is this what you really want? Allow yourself to trust in your intuition, rather than your logical mind.

-29-

Know Your Worth

29. Know Your Worth

Knowing your worth is your internal measure of how you value yourself regardless of what other people might think of you or say about you. When you know your real value it's easier to speak up for yourself and stand up for what is right even when others don't agree with you. Self-worth is the opinion you have about yourself and the value you place on yourself. It is your belief that you are a good person who deserves good things. Knowing your true worth takes courage and makes life decisions much clearer.

As I began modeling, I participated in some fashion shows for "exposure" (meaning free). Some companies and brands had money to pay for the models, but why would they pay when these models would do it for free for "exposure"?

During this time I did not request a payment because I was excited to be a part of these events. I looked at it as an investment. Some were even for charities, which I greatly support. After this, I finally started receiving booked jobs. I started to see my worth and stopped modeling for "exposure."

There was a bridal fashion show coming up on Sunday. Sunday is what I call my "Jesus Day" which means that I rest, and appreciate what God has created. I was curious about the job so I asked. A bridal store was offering $100 for a model for a whole day of work and travel. Come on, now this is beyond low, but some models did it, again for "exposure." You are what you invest your time in, and experience goes a long way, but this is definitely not me anymore, especially working on Sunday.

I have been contacted through social media by brands to collaborate together. I sent them an invoice of how my payments look and the requirements I request. As soon as they see this they do not contact me, and that is ok because I always tell myself that this is not meant to be.

I look at it as a small opportunity that passed me by and when one door closes a bigger and better one opens. And it did.

I was contacted by the photographers for the Moxy Hotel. They were doing a photo shoot for the Moxy Hotel in downtown Boston. I set my price, sent it over, and BOOM, I was booked. I knew my worth and I knew I was worth working for big names and receiving a bigger payment.

No more free collaborations. No more free work for exposure. I stood by my values and walked away from companies and people who could not afford to work with me. My time became valuable.

I developed my status as a high-end model working for well-known brand names and began appearing in commercials, movies, and tv series. I had brands pay for my hotel stays and travel. Once I knew my worth I was only getting bigger, I was more respected because I respected myself and my time, and I was making more money working with top, high-paying brands.

As I found value in myself, I also wanted others to find value in themselves, especially women. I used to be that woman that "settled" because I was just happy and excited to be a part of the modeling industry and receive the bare minimum. With every opportunity and lesson I received from this experience, my standards only became higher. I started to see the value in myself and I never settled until I got what I wanted and what I deserved.

When conducting any type of work, know that you are a valuable asset to an industry. Whether you work at an office job or have a business of your own, know your own worth because your skills, time, and talents are valuable.

 *Exercise*

What is one action you can take today that would help you value your worth more?

Write this action down below.

-30-

Celebrate the New You

Step 30 - Celebrate the New You

Congratulations! You made it to the end of the book. Now celebrate yourself. You did the hard work. You may have gone through turmoil, turbulence, heartbreak, pain, happiness, being alone, crying, and frustration, but you were patient with yourself and made it to the other side. You have made it to the side of success, whatever that may look like for you.

Now, you are ready. Ready to receive everything you ever wanted. Ready for all the abundance, prosperity, love, joy, and new beginnings.

I love celebrating myself, because who else could have been there for me if it wasn't for me? A lot of people have asked me, "How have you been through all of this and stay sane?"

I have my purpose. As long as I am alive, and able to have a voice I will use my stories and tools to inspire and help others. As long as God gave me another day to live, I have to keep going, for myself, for my children, and for you. Anything and everything is possible if you only believe. If you believe you shall receive.

It is time to take that champagne bottle you have been saving and go ahead and bless yourself and celebrate. You are finally the person you have always wanted to become and I am so happy and grateful that I was there to take you every step of the way.

May God bless you. Remember you made it this far, what's stopping you from going even further? Go ahead and take the next step into your dream life—you are ready to receive!

About the Author

Angelika Kilian was born in Poland and moved to America when she was six years old. Staying true to her Polish roots, she is now a dual citizen of the United States and Poland. Standing at 5' 10" with exotic Polish features, she was quickly scouted over a decade ago by Moet & Chandon to be a model for one of their campaigns. Since then, Angelika has modeled for a diverse group of big names in print and runway. Modeling opened doors to being cast in movies and commercials.

Besides being in the entertainment industry, Angelika was the first member of her family to graduate from college with a Bachelor's degree in Economics from UMASS Boston.

Her greatest passion is to make the world a better place with her inspiring stories and teachings. She does this for those around her and those she has never met. She is devoted to using her platform to help people and give back to society through charitable causes and shedding light on normalizing mental health and abusive struggles. She believes that being exactly who you are is enough, and you can overcome and do anything you put your mind to.

www.ingramcontent.com/pod-product-compliance
Lightning Source LLC
Chambersburg PA
CBHW051527120626
46551CB00012B/1110